Catherine le Galley   May 2007

The Good Dog Library

Dog Care & Nutrition

Care, Feeding, and Grooming Advice to Bring Out the Best in Your Dog

ISBN: 0-9758716-2-5

Tufts Media Enterprises
200 Boston Ave., Suite 3500
Medford, MA 02155 USA

Dog Care & Nutrition
Care, Feeding, and Grooming Advice
to Bring Out the Best in Your Dog

ISBN: 0-9758716-2-5
1. Dogs-Nutrition   2. Dogs-Care   3. Dogs-Grooming
4. Canine   5. Canine Nutrition
6. Canine Care Canine-Grooming

Manufactured in the United States of America

The Good Dog Library

Dog Care & Nutrition

Care, Feeding, and Grooming Advice to Bring Out the Best in Your Dog

Scientific Editor: John Berg

Veterinary Surgeon and Chair, Department of Clinical Sciences
Tufts Cummings School of Veterinary Medicine
North Grafton, MA

Contents

Section II: Grooming

Section III: Nutrition

Introduction

Becoming a dog owner carries with it an awesome responsibility—and a blizzard of choices to make about your pet's care, nutrition, and grooming. Do you really need to brush your dog's teeth? Is it true that you shouldn't bathe him or her too often? And how do you pick a dog food, given the number of options at any grocery or pet store?

The experts of Tufts University School of Veterinary Medicine, one of the premier veterinary schools in the United States, are here to help. In this book, *Dog Care and Nutrition*, we guide you through the sometimes bewildering and contradictory information that dog owners face.

Test your dog IQ with the quiz in the first chapter; then in the second chapter, chuckle at the things we do for our dogs, such as leaving the television or radio on for them while we're gone and talking baby talk to them when we're home.

The Care section then takes on a more serious tone, providing clear, practical advice on brushing your dog's teeth (yes, you should do it); dealing with hot spots; and controlling fleas, ticks, mosquitoes, and other undesirables who at best are a nuisance and at worst carry diseases that threaten your pet's life. This section includes share down-to-earth advice on care situations that you can handle at home—and those that require immediate attention from a veterinarian.

You'll find information on how to find the best option for you and your pet when you're leaving town and he or she can't come along as well as recommendations on how to make car travel comfortable and safe for your dog. And, we'll share ways you can improve the odds that a missing pet will find his or her way back to your pack.

The Grooming section features advice on bathing (it's an old wives tale that once a year may be too much) and your dog and tending the the animal's other needs. You'll find expert help on what to do if you cut your pet's nails too close, and learn why it's a good thing if the dog's footpads are rough and tough.

Finally, the Nutrition section explains how to feed your dog a balanced diet—and shares why raw foods are not the answer to dog health and preservatives are not the villains. You'll also learn how to tell when your dog is obese, and how to help him or her lose weight if necessary.

Becoming a dog owner is an awesome responsibility—and brings with it awesome rewards. Congratulations on joining the dog owner pack! ■

John Berg
Veterinary Surgeon & Chair, Department of Clinical Sciences
Tufts University School of Veterinary Medicine

Section I

Care

1

How Dog Smart Are You?

Take our quiz to see just how much you know about being a good, responsible dog owner.

Perhaps you're the owner of a new pup or a longtime caretaker of a dog who's earned a place as a member of the family. In either case, you may question if you're providing the best nutrition. You wonder if a hot, dry nose means your dog is under the weather. And when exactly is the ideal time to neuter that new puppy?

Not to worry. You've come to the right place for help. We've compiled a wealth of questions about dogs' health and behavior.

The answers will boost your canine know-how and just might improve your dog's life. Cozy up with your furry companion and get started. Look on page 16 for answers, explanations, and scoring information. Then, read this book to get the answers you need on dog care and nutrition.

The Questions

1. How many teeth does a dog have?

2. What's a dog's average temperature?

3. Does a hot, dry nose indicate illness?

4. How often do unspayed dogs go into heat?

5. How many puppies will a medium-size dog deliver?

6. Should you allow your dog to have a litter of puppies to satisfy her maternal instinct before spaying?

7. What's the optimal age for neutering?

8. True or false: You judge a dog's condition by looking into his or her eyes.

9. Is eating grass normal or a sign of illness?

10. True or false: A dog's licking or chewing houseplants is harmless.

11. How long should a dog have diarrhea before you seek medical help?

12. True or false: Arthritis, a normal part of aging, has no cure.

13. How many calories a day does a twenty-pound dog under eight years of age require for good health?
  a. 350 to 450
  b. 600 to 800
  c. 1,000 to 1,200

14. How many times a day should you feed a dog?

15. What information should you look for on a dog food label to ensure the best nutrition?
  a. The food's percentage of water
  b. Certification it meets Association of American Feed Control Officials' (AAFCO) requirements for feeding trials
  c. The expiration date

16. What's the most common dietary problem among dogs?

17. True or false: Dogs can hear sounds up to 250 yards away.

18. True or false: Dogs are color-blind.

19. True or false: Behavior problems are the top reason for dog abandonment.

20. True or false: You come home to find an expensive pair of shoes or one of your child's toys chewed beyond recognition. Punishing your puppy now is the best way to prevent repetition of the behavior.

21. Based on an eleven-year life span, the average cost of owning a dog is:
   a. $13,350
   b. $5,350
   c. $2,500

22. Dogs originated from:
   a. Wolves
   b. Jackals
   c. Coyotes and wolves

23. What's the most popular dog breed in the United States?
   a. Labrador Retriever
   b. Poodle
   c. German Shepherd

24. What breed doesn't bark?
   a. Papillion
   b. Shar-Pei
   c. Basenji

25. What's the smallest breed?
   a. Chihuahua
   b. Yorkshire Terrier
   c. Miniature Pinscher

The Answers

Here are answers and some accompanying explanations to the quiz.

1. Dogs have twenty-eight deciduous, or baby, teeth, and forty-two permanent teeth. They lose their needle-sharp baby teeth at four months.

2. The average canine temperature is 100-102 degrees Fahrenheit, much higher than humans' 98.6.

3. *No.* This is a myth. "Certainly, a dehydrated pet will often have dry nose as well as dry mouth, sunken eyes and look 'sick,'" says Michael Stone, a veterinary internist at Tufts University School of Veterinary Medicine. "However, many normal dogs have dry noses." It's common for older dogs to develop callus-like thickening on their noses. And many dogs with wet noses can be seriously ill, so don't be misled. If your dog's nose is dry, but he or she is eating and behaving normally, don't be alarmed. If your dog has a wet nose but lacks an appetite, appears listless or shows other sign of illness, take the animal to the veterinarian.

4. Most females go into heat twice yearly. Some dogs cycle only annually.

5. The average number is about four to eight puppies. Miniature breeds may have only one puppy while giant breeds can have fifteen or more.

6. *No.* It serves no purpose to allow a dog to have a litter of pups before spaying. In fact, failing to spay or neuter contributes to pet overpopulation and the resulting euthanasia of millions of dogs annually. Females suffer no adverse affects from not having puppies.

7. Spaying females before their first heat at six to nine months of age is optimum. "For male dogs, the best age is unknown. Anytime after they've reached a safe age for anesthesia—at approximately ten weeks of age—is appropriate," Dr. Stone says. Some veterinarians advise it's best to neuter males before they develop characteristic behaviors, such as marking territory with urine. Many veterinarians neuter both male and female dogs routinely at approximately six months of age. A move is also under way among other veterinarians and shelters to spay and neuter pups much earlier, in the six- to eight-week range, which has helped decrease the number of unwanted animals.

8. *True.* Dogs' eyes provide a valuable window for gauging their health. Some dogs suffer from constant tearing, which may be normal for them. In others, tearing can be a sign of a sinus or upper respiratory infection. A cloudy bluing of the eye is an early sign of hepatitis. A pale color in the normally pink membrane around the eye could indicate anemia. If a dog feels rundown, the eyes may lose their glossiness.

9. Dogs commonly eat grass, but it's not known whether they do so to make themselves vomit or whether the grass makes them vomit. Dogs seem to like the consistency of grass, but you should discourage them from eating it. Grass itself may be harmless but could be coated with harmful chemicals, pesticides or parasite eggs.

10. *False.* Many common houseplants are poisonous to dogs, including holly, English ivy, hydrangea, Christmas rose, poinsettia and rhododendron. If your dog eats a plant and you're unsure if it's poisonous, check with a poison control center. Treat all poisonings as emergencies and get prompt veterinary attention. The American Society for the Prevention of Cruelty to Animals (ASPCA) Animal Poison Control Center has an emergency hot line that provides round-the-clock telephone help. It's available at (888) 4ANIHELP for a forty-five dollar consultation fee.

11. *Two days.* Withhold a meal or two and provide plenty of water so your dog doesn't become dehydrated. Ask the veterinarian if you should feed bland foods, such as poached chicken and rice, for a few days until your dog returns to normal.

12. *True*, but ask the veterinarian about medications that can ease your dog's pain. Provide reasonable regular exercise and consider alternatives like gentle massage of the affected areas.

13. *b. 600 to 800 calories.* Requirements vary with age and activity level. "Dogs less than eight years of age should average 60 to 80 calories per kilogram (2.2 pounds) of body weight per day; dogs greater than eight often require less, in the 40 to 60 calories per kilogram of weight per day range," Dr. Stone says. How-

ever, active dogs require more calories than sedentary ones. Check with the veterinarian to determine the best nutrition for your dog.

14. After approximately one year of age, feeding once daily is adequate for most dogs, says Dr. Stone. Some, especially smaller breeds, eat twice per day. Some owners feed ad libitum—at the dog's pleasure, with food in the bowl all the time.

15. Feed only food certified as meeting requirements based upon the AAFCO feeding trials. "Pet food companies concerned about their product will have their food tested and prominently display this acceptance on their packaging, if present," Dr. Stone says. AAFCO, at **www.aafco.org**, is a national organization that regulates the manufacture, distribution and sale of animal feeds. It also licenses food that meets AAFCO nutrient analysis, but this isn't as desirable as feeding trials. In the nutrient analysis studies, food is chemically analyzed for content. During feeding trials, the food is fed to dogs, and they're regularly monitored.

16. Obesity is the most common dietary problem, especially in affluent areas. "I would guess close to 80 percent of my canine patients are portly," Dr. Stone says.

17. *True*. Dogs can hear sounds more accurately than humans—from as far as 250 yards. Most people can't hear beyond 25 yards. The human ear can detect sound waves vibrating at frequencies up to twenty thousand times a second. Dogs can hear sound waves vibrating at frequencies of more than thirty thousand times per second.

18. *False*. Dogs can see color but not in as vivid a color scheme as we do. Their vision compares to ours at twilight. How do scientists know? One way they use is to shine beams of colored lights into dogs' eyes and analyze the spectrum—the pattern of light—reflected back. They compare results with the pattern produced when they shine the same lights into human eyes.

19. *True*. "The most common reasons given are that the dog's too active, barks too much or is destructive," Dr. Stone says. In many cases owners really didn't want the dog and may consider normal behavior a problem. "Veterinarians do owe pets and owners advice about how to avoid behavior problems, and these are best addressed at young age, when the dog is most trainable," he says.

20. *False*. Your puppy—or an adult dog for that matter—won't understand the connection between punishment and the shoe he chewed hours before. In fact, responsible trainers today don't use punishment. Instead, they reinforce positive behavior. The only time you should correct your dog for inappropriate chewing is when you catch him in the act. Even then, only say "No! Leave it!" and take the item away. Remember, puppies use early chewing to begin shedding baby teeth. Provide a variety of appropriate chew toys.

21. *a. $13,350.* The Avery County Humane Society in Newland, North Carolina, estimated this cost, including food, veterinary preventive care, training, spaying or neutering, licensing fees and miscellaneous expenses.

22. *a. Wolves.* A University of California Los Angeles study, analyzing wolf, coyote and jackal DNA, found that dogs evolved from wolves and have no ancestry among jackals or coyotes.

23. *a. Labrador Retriever.* The gentle, easygoing breed tops the list of American Kennel Club registrations, followed by Goldens, German Shepherds, Dachshunds and Beagles.

24. *c. Basenji.*

25. *a. Chihuahua*. Full-grown, this lively and intelligent breed weighs six pounds or less.

How You Rate

Take a free pass on No. 9 and award yourself one point for whatever answer you gave. No one knows why dogs eat grass. Give yourself one point for each correct answer on the other questions. Add them up to see how you fared. If you scored a nearly impossible perfect 25, congratulations! You're a world-class dog owner.

15 to 24: You're best of show.

10 to 15: Still a champ. This was a tough quiz.

10 or below: Woof! At least you were concerned enough about dog welfare to take the test—and buy this book! ■

2

What We Do for Our Dogs!

*Do you view your canine companion
as a friend or part of your family?
You have plenty of company!*

Considering that our dogs freely give us unconditional loyalty, protection, entertainment, and much-needed diversion from life's stresses, it's no wonder owners go to great lengths to make life healthy and happy for their dogs. In today's society, there are more and more single, childless adults, and the very definition of family may be changing. It's not as common as it once was to live close to extended family and as a result, our pets become more and more important in our lives.

By the Numbers

Sixty-two percent of U.S. households own at least one pet; 40 percent own at least one dog, according to the American Pet Products Manufacturers Association. Most dog households have one dog (63 percent; 24 percent have two dogs and 13 percent own three or more). Twenty percent of these dogs came from an animal shelter.

The majority of primary pet caregivers in the United States are women (58 percent), according to research by Bayer Corp., whose Animal Health unit conducts research and and develops medical products for companion and farm animals. Dog owners outnumber cat owners (42 percent versus 31 percent; cat owners tend to own more than one cat) and 17 percent of households own both a cat and a dog.

Bayer's research found that 73 percent of pet owners consider themselves, their spouse or a member of the household to be a "pet parent." Households with children are more likely to own a cat or dog (64 percent versus 51 percent of childless households). Ninety-three percent consider their pet to be a member of the family.

Top concerns include caring for the pet's overall health and caring for the pet's comfort and happiness (95 percent each); going to the vet for regular checkups and vaccinations (86 percent); providing flea control (80 percent); and providing pet identification (74 percent), according to Bayer.

Dollars and Sense

Americans spend $31 billion annually on pet products, more than they spend on toys for humans or candy, the American Pet Products Manufacturers Association says. Sixty percent of dog, cat, bird and small animal owners have bought a gift for their pet.

Enriched Environments

Many owners provide creative forms of stimulation for dogs they must leave home alone from time to time. Such environmental enrichment often takes the form of leaving televisions and radios on. Tufts University School of Veterinary Medicine took an informal poll and found that classical music and talk shows are the most popular listening choices. (But please keep the volume down, because dogs have much more acute hearing than we do.)

To provide even more realistic "company," you could play a continuous-loop audiotape of household voices and noises for your dog when he or she is alone, suggests Dr. Nicholas Dodman, director of the Behavior Clinic at Tufts University School of Veterinary Medicine.

Dogs are ever interested in what's going on around them. If your dog is not excessively protective or predatory, give your home-alone canine opportunities to look outside. To facilitate this, move a step stool or piece of furniture (one that can withstand some wear, tear, and hair!) close to a closed and screened window. Some owners have even been known to build in dog-friendly windows.

Leash walking is ordinarily one of the best ways to exercise and stimulate your dog, but sometimes this commonplace activity is a bit more complicated than one would expect. Dr. Linda Ross, asso-

ciate professor and internist at Tufts University School of Veterinary Medicine, tells of one owner who adopted a dog with a congenital heart defect, which made even mild exercise risky. "When this woman walks her group of dogs, she puts the one with the heart condition in a baby stroller," says Dr. Ross.

How far would you go? Well, informal polls by SitStay.com, a dog supplies company, show that most owners have made major modifications at home to accommodate their dogs (65.32 percent); own dogs with allergies (55.43 percent), which can require an investment in medication and modifying human behavior, such as smoking; and talk baby talk to their dogs (75.47 percent).

Behavioral Bonuses

Some owners who have dogs with behavioral problems go to great (and innovative) lengths to help their pets. In the title chapter of his book *The Dog Who Loved Too Much: Tales, Treatments, and the Psychology of Dogs* (Bantam), Dr. Dodman recounts the story of Elsa, a Labrador retriever with separation anxiety. To help Elsa handle solitude more calmly, her resourceful owner made a continuous-loop

audiotape of himself issuing obedience commands and enthusiastic praise. He then added a voice-activated circuit so the tape ran only when Elsa began whimpering with anxiety. When Elsa heard her owner's voice, she calmed down.

The Results Are In

According to a recent survey conducted by the American Animal Hospital Association, owners of home-alone pets go to great lengths to assure their animals' comfort and safety. Specifically:

■ *60 percent of pet owners leave the air conditioner or fan on.*

■ *50 percent leave toys out for their pets.*

■ *41 percent leave lights on.*

■ *32 percent turn on the TV or radio.*

■ *30 percent open windows or blinds.*

Medical Management

Many owners go the extra mile, emotionally and financially to help dogs manage chronic, incurable canine conditions like epilepsy and diabetes. Even less-serious chronic conditions, such as allergies, move some owners to take extraordinary measures like removing carpet to cut down on dust mites.

Indeed, the American Pet Products Manufacturers Association says that dog owners spend an average $196 annually on veterinary-related expenses; 70 percent of owned dogs are spayed or neutered.

The American Veterinary Medical Association says that 84 percent of dog-owning households made at least one veterinary visit in 2001. Within that group, 22 percent made one visit; 24 percent, two visits; and 38 percent, three visits. Vaccinations were the reason for most visits.

Special Menus

Owners also often make culinary accommodations for their dogs. Every day, Dr. Bruce Fogle, a London-based veterinarian, prepares rotisserie chicken and fettucine with olive oil for his fourteen-year-old Golden retriever, Liberty, whose heart condition has led to appetite loss and cardiac cachexia—severe muscle wasting. While he does his best to balance the nutrients in this homemade diet, Dr. Fogle is more concerned that Libby eats than he is with concocting a completely balanced diet—a greater concern if Libby were a younger dog with a longer life expectancy. The biggest problem: friends sometimes find the dog's food in the fridge and unwittingly eat it.

Creature Comforts

Sometimes, we take special measures just to make canine life more pleasurable. When selecting cars, dog people often place greater stock in easy canine access and their dog's interior-space requirements than they do in power and styling. (Some owners even bring their dogs along for test drives.)

If you think you or a friend has gone overboard with catering to a dog, consider the story of a couple who set up four beds for their arthritic Saint Bernard. And when the husband was assembling a workbench in the garage, he purposely left off the lower shelf to avoid interfering with the big dog's favorite snoozing spot. And then there's the owner who paid her housecleaner extra to perform a slightly unusual task—vacuuming the dog, who relished that kind of grooming.

And what do we get out of all this pampering? Happiness. Ninety-seven percent of pet owners surveyed by the American Animal Hospital Association said their pet made them smile at least once a day, and 76 percent said their pet eases stress. How do you put a price on that? ■

3

How Safe
Is Your Home?

*Check out these ten ways to reduce
toxins in and around your house.*

Admit it: if you thought that conditions in your house were dangerous to your health, you would change them or move. And yet many of us expose our beloved canine friends to life-threatening toxins and life-shortening conditions every day.

Many of the dangers lurk in products we use casually, without knowledge of their effects on our dogs. Ironically, while some of these conditions are potential threats to our own health as well, we often fail to consider them until they wreak havoc with the vitality of one of our animals.

Many of these hazards are chemical in nature. Exposed on a daily basis, our pets bear ever-increasing loads of toxins, from the lawns and yards they romp that are often treated with pesticides and fertilizers, to the sidewalks and streets where we walk them, and, too often, even to the very rugs and floors on which they lie in our own homes. Some veterinarians believe that this constant bombardment of toxins is unhealthy and may contribute to some health problems seen in today's dogs.

Fortunately, we can easily improve the health conditions in our homes. We've compiled a list of ten commonly found household health hazards. Reducing your dog's, and your own, exposure to as many of them as possible can improve both of your healths, and maybe even extend your lives together.

Toxic Cleaners

If used in total accordance with the cautions on their labels, few household cleaners are dangerous to your dog. The problem is that many people never read or ignore the labels. Never mind that this is a violation of federal law—what you don't know can hurt your dog. Our first recommendation: **Read the label**.

A note about hazard warnings: If the hazard statement begins with "Caution" or "Warning," it signals that the product is not likely to produce permanent damage as a result of exposure, if appropriate first aid is given. If the hazard statement begins with "Danger," it indicates that even greater precautions should be taken, since accidental exposure or ingestion could cause tissue damage. Examine the labels of all your household products to determine the level of caution you should employ when using the product—or whether to even use it at all.

> 66 REDUCING YOUR DOG'S, AND YOUR OWN, EXPOSURE TO AS MANY TOXINS AS POSSIBLE CAN IMPROVE THE HEALTH OF BOTH OF YOU AND YOUR DOG, AND MAYBE EVEN EXTEND YOUR LIVES TOGETHER. 99

To avoid accidentally poisoning your dog, never leave a bucket or bowl containing any cleaning solution unattended. If you mix cleaners into any container that resembles one your dog has drunk from, make sure you empty and rinse it well before you walk out of sight. If you pour bleach or other cleaners into your toilet bowl, make sure you close the lid or tightly close the door to the bathroom so that your dog cannot enter.

Never mix cleaning products. Products that are safe when used alone can sometimes become dangerous when mixed with other products. A common mishap occurs when people unwittingly mix products containing bleach (sodium hypochlorite) with products containing ammonia or acids. Such mixtures will release highly dangerous gases.

Read the labels of all your household products to determine the level of caution you should employ when using the product—or whether you should use it at all.

The safest approach to housecleaning? Look for products that carry the "Green Seal of Approval." To earn a green seal, a product must pass rigorous tests and meet the most stringent environmental standards. Green Seal products must demonstrably reduce air and water pollution, cut the waste of energy and natural resources, slow ozone depletion and the risk of global warming, prevent toxic contamination, and protect fish and wildlife and their habitats.

Poisonous Plants

Many common house and garden plants are highly poisonous if consumed. Few dogs eat plants, but you never know! Bored or agitated canines have done strange things. The following plants are dangerous to dogs: **All plant parts: Azaleas, buttercup, calla lily, laurels, rhododendron, tiger lily, philodendrons, poinsettia, mistletoe. Bulbs: crocus, daffodil, tulip. Berries: Christmas berry, jasmine, red sage.**

The best course is to eliminate poisonous plants from your home decorating and landscaping plans.

Cigarette Smoke

Everyone knows about the dangers of secondhand smoke for humans. But not everyone has thought about it enough to realize that cigarette smoke is just as dangerous to dogs as it is to humans. If you don't want to shorten your dog's life, consider quitting or smoking outdoors only. Ask guests to smoke outside, too.

Hazardous Chewable Items

If you have a teething puppy or a dog who has gotten into the habit of chewing odd items, you should dog-proof his or her environment as stringently as you would for a baby. While it is impossible to eliminate every single item that might be dangerous if chewed, remove all the likely suspects from the animal's reach: electric cords, medicines, cleaners, and chemical containers. If the dog cannot be kept under observation, he or she should be contained in a puppy pen or crate with a few appropriate chew toys.

Chemical Flea Controls

Fleas are annoying. They can make you and your dog nearly crazy with itching, transmit larvae for tapeworms, and aggravate allergies. But when we're locked in a battle for control over a rampant flea population, we tend to go overboard, enlisting the aid of any and every chemical known to science—pet sprays, collars, shampoos, powders, dips, and tablets as well as chemical sprays applied to our rugs, floors, and even yards.

Unfortunately, many of the products on the market can be quite toxic, especially if instructions on the label are not followed closely. Organochlorines, found in some flea dips and shampoos, can cause exaggerated responses to touch, light and sound as well as spasms, muscle tremors, and seizures. Carbamates, found in dips, collars, powders, and sprays, can cause profuse salivation, muscular twitching, slowed pulse, labored breathing, vomiting, watery eyes, and paralysis, to name but a few symptoms. Pyrethrins are the least toxic chemicals commonly used in flea shampoos and sprays; they are safe for dogs, but not cats. Many of the most recently developed flea control products whose active ingredients include fipronyl, selanectin, and inidaclopril are very safe for dogs.

Read the labels carefully. When a label tells you to avoid getting the product on your own skin, to wash it off quickly and thoroughly, to avoid breathing the fumes, and to dispose of the empty container in a certain manner, it's telling you that the product is really not that "safe." Can it really be "harmless" for your dog?

Dirty Water

Plenty of fresh, clean, cool drinking water must always be available to your dog. Dehydration can cause and worsen many other health conditions. An ample supply of good water, on the other hand, can help the dog's body shed environmental toxins.

To ensure your dog wants to drink enough water, put the bowl in a cool, protected place where dust and debris won't fall in it; keep the bowl clean; and keep the water fresh and cool. If your tap water smells bad or contains any substances that have moved you to buy pure drinking water for your family, consider providing the same water for your dog.

Garden Chemicals

Dogs absorb insecticides, herbicides, and fungicides from the soil by walking, lying, and rolling on it. They are also exposed to many potent insecticides in the home such as ant, roach, or fly sprays. Long-term overexposure may increase the animal's chances of suffering from cancer, allergies, and kidney and liver problems.

Outside, use native species of plants in your garden; they will naturally resist many local pests. Alternatively, plant disease-resistant strains of plants, flowers, trees, and vegetables, available at most nurseries. The health of these strains is less dependent on the use of chemicals. Use "friendly" enemies of pests, like ladybugs, that hungrily consume the aphids that plague roses and other plants. Ask your neighbors about their pesticide use, and let them know about your most successful organic gardening techniques.

Also, if you have to use solvent, paints, or harsh cleaners in your home or garage, dispose of the waste by soaking it up with rags, sand, or cat litter, and place those materials in a garbage can. Don't just sweep or hose the chemicals into the soil or onto the lawn. Contrary to appearances, the chemicals don't just disappear.

Indoors, use good housekeeping practices to control pests. Keep floors and counters wiped clean and empty your kitchen garbage can frequently.

Air Fresheners

Contrary to popular belief, commercial air and carpet deodorizers don't work by removing the odor from the air or carpet. Rather, they use strong perfumes to overwhelm odors such as cigarette smoke or strong food smells. That's why after some time, the perfume or scent that masked the problem dissipates and the offensive smell "returns."

To genuinely freshen a room's odor, sprinkle baking soda liberally on carpets. Vacuum it up after thirty minutes or so. Vanilla extract, poured into a shallow dish on a high shelf where your dog can't reach it, can make a room smell good.

Carpet Shampoo

Most formulas of carpet cleaning liquids contain either perchlorethylene, a known carcinogen that damages the nervous system and liver and kidney tissues, or ammonium hydroxide, a corrosive agent that is extremely irritating to eyes, skin, and respiratory passages.

If you rent a carpet cleaner, try using plain hot water, which works very well all by itself to remove dirt and odors from rugs. You'll probably be amazed at the amount of soap suds in the dirty water you empty from the cleaning tank when you're done. These residues are evidence of the chemicals that have lurked in the carpet since the last time it was cleaned.

Lack of an Emergency Plan

Natural disasters can and do strike anywhere, anytime. In the mass confusion following a fire, earthquake, flood, mud slide, snowstorm, or hurricane, our animal friends can easily get lost or separated. Another disaster can happen if any of the above calamities cuts off your food and water supply. We all remember all too well the tragedy of September 11, 2001; a senseless act orchestrated from beyond our borders can change our lives forever. While many of us developed emergency plans for contacting loved ones, are those plans still up to date—and do they include the dogs?

Store provisions for your pets along with your family's emergency supplies. Disaster preparedness experts recommend keeping at least a two-week supply of food and water for both the humans and animals in the house. Canned and dry foods should be stored in a cool, dry place. Be sure to check the dated shelf life, occasionally buying new stocks and using the stored goods. Keep at least ten gallons of water on hand, rotating and using the bottles so that none are stored for more than a couple of months. If you are ordered to evacuate your home, do not assume you will be back soon. Heed the orders of disaster officials, of course, but take your dog with you if at all possible.

Having identification on your animal friend may be his or her only chance to be returned to you in case of a disaster. Even if the phone (or even the house at the address!) listed on your dog's ID tags is missing after a disaster, the information can be used by rescuers to reunite you with your beloved friend. It can also be a good idea to keep a good photo of your dog with your most important papers, the kind of papers you'd grab first if you had to run out of your house in an emergency. The photo should clearly show the dog's size and markings. ■

4

The Bug Battle

What's the best way to fight fleas, ticks, heartworm, and other problems caused by insects, arachnids, and parasites? By preventing the problems in the first place.

Every dog owner knows that getting rid of fleas can be one of the biggest challenges of dog-keeping. It's a challenge that must be dealt with; fleas can make your dog—and you and members of your family—miserable through their tiny but painful bites. Further, some dogs and people develop allergic reactions to flea saliva. The bites also can cause a skin condition, flea allergy dermatitis, and fleas can be carriers of the tapeworm parasite.

And fleas aren't the only bugs your dog faces outdoors. Ticks, mites, wasps, bees, scorpions, and spiders all pose potential risks to your dog's health. Then there's the ubiquitous mosquito, which can transmit heartworm disease. What should you do?

Fleas

Fleas are prolific, producing thousands of eggs during their three- to four-month lifespan. In ideal conditions, the cycle takes just two weeks from egg-laying (the female can lay as many as fifty eggs in a single day and starts laying eggs within a day of landing on your dog) to larvae to pupae to hatched fleas capable of laying eggs of their own. And, fleas can live from twelve days to six months.

Depending on where you live, flea season can be a year-round problem or limited to four or so months annually. They thrive in warm, humid weather. The U.S. Food and Drug Administration estimates there are more than two hundred species of fleas in this country. The American Veterinary Medicine Association estimates that flea-related diseases account for 35 percent of visits to all small animal veterinary practices and 50 percent of all skin problems veterinarians see.

The best way to fight fleas is to protect your dog before an infestation, and that doesn't mean a flea collar.

"In the general, the efficacy of flea collars is very low," says Gene Nesbitt, a clinical professor at Tufts University School of Veterinary Medicine. Topical "spot on" preventatives are much better at battling fleas, effective more than 95 percent of the time. If your dog swims every day, the efficacy of even an excellent topical preventative will be lower.

If you've been following an effective flea control program and your dog still becomes infested, that's a sign that there's been a break in your program, such as a change in environment, Dr. Nesbitt says.

The Signs
Fleas, often the size of a sesame seed, can be difficult if not impossible to spot. Often, all you'll see is their dark droppings left on the dog's coat. Just because you don't see fleas leaping from your dog when he or she is combed does not mean the animal doesn't have fleas.

Other signs can include bumps on the dog's groin and abdomen; hair loss; and crusting and scabbing of sores, particularly in the lumbar region of the animal's back.

The Treatment
If you and your vet have established that your dog has fleas, Dr. Nesbitt recommends Novartis' Capstar, given orally in tablet form, to get rid of the insects. "There's a quick knockdown; in an hour, 90 percent of the fleas will be off, but there is no residual effect," he says. That means that if you don't rid the environment of fleas, they'll be right back on your dog.

"The best solution is a good flea bath and initiation of a permanent, continuous flea control program," Dr. Nesbitt says. He stresses the importance of treating all animals in the household, even those who don't show signs of fleas. Otherwise, the insects can lay eggs deep in carpets and rugs, in pet and pet owner's beds, and elsewhere in the house, resulting in a vicious circle of infestation.

It's important to give those areas of your home a thorough cleaning as well. Vacuum carpets and rugs frequently, and vacuum or wash your pet's bedding regularly. Change vacuum bags frequently and burn the used one if there's been a recent infestation.

Ticks

Ticks are arachnids like mites, spiders, and scorpions. Females lay from a hundred to as many as six thousand eggs at a time depending on the species. Their life cycle is from eggs to larvae to nymphs to adults, and the lifespan of an individual tick can range from less than a year to several years depending on the species. About two hundred species are found in the United States, according to the FDA. Ticks require a blood meal at each stage following hatching.

Ticks are generally found in wooded areas, but even urban areas are not tick-free. They prefer moist, shaded areas and are most prevalent in the late spring and summer. Ticks are most likely to be found in the East, Midwest, Texas, and the Pacific Northwest.

An engorged tick eventually will fall from the dog's body, but that doesn't mean the danger is over.

"Once the tick takes a blood meal, then there's potential for infection of Lyme disease," Dr. Nesbitt says. Lyme, carried by deer ticks, can cause lameness and arthritic symptoms in dogs. (Dogs cannot directly transmit the disease to people.) Ixodid, or hard, ticks, carry Rocky Mountain Spotted Fever and can infect both dogs and humans. The disease's symptoms can include fever and muscle pain, followed by development of rash, according to the Centers for Disease Control and Prevention; early diagnosis can be difficult and the disease can be fatal if it is not treated.

The Signs

While a tick is still on your dog's body, it's easy to spot. The eight-legged bug's body swells up with the blood it sucks from the dog. It can take a tick a day or two to fully latch to your pet, which means it's extremely important for you to thoroughly check your dog's body when he or she has been in an environment conducive to ticks.

The Treatment

If you find a tick on your dog, the treatment is basic: remove the tick. Do not try to burn it out with a match or cigarette lighter. That's an old wives' tale, as is the caution that you must not leave the tick's head in your dog's body. "I've never seen a head left in," Dr. Nesbitt says. Tweezers can be used to remove the tick. Clean the resulting wound so that it doesn't become infected.

As is the case with fleas, prevention is preferable. It's important to keep in mind that the goal of many excellent tick control products is to kill the tick before it attaches to your dog, not to prevent the tick from jumping on your dog in the first place. "Some medications get a bad rap," Dr. Nesbitt says. "Your dog can come in with live ticks. The question is whether the tick attaches or not."

Quick Tips

The American Veterinary Medicine Association provides these recommendations for dealing with ticks and fleas.

- *Look for fleas, ticks, and coat abnormalities any time you groom your dog or cat.*

- *See your veterinarian if your pet excessively scratches, chews, or licks his or her haircoat, or persistently shakes his or her head. These clinical signs may indicate the presence of external parasites or other conditions requiring medical care.*

- *Prompt treatment of parasites lessens your pet's discomfort, decreases the chances of disease transmission from parasite to pet, and may reduce the degree of home infestation.*

- *Discuss the health of all family pets with your veterinarian when one pet becomes infested. Some parasites cycle among pets, making control of infestations difficult unless other pets are considered.*

- *Tell your veterinarian if you have attempted any parasite remedies.*

- *Leave treatment to the experts. Your veterinarian offers technical expertise and can assist you in identifying products that are most likely to effectively and safely control your pet's parasite problem.*

Numerous brochures about dog care are available for purchase at the association's Web site, www.awma.org.

Mosquitoes

To humans, mosquito bites are an annoyance. To dogs, if the mosquito is carrying the heartworm disease, the bite can be deadly.

The cycle begins when a mosquito bites an infected animal and takes in blood that contains young heartworms, called microfilariae. When the mosquito bites another animal, the microfilariae then are released into the second animal's bloodstream. Typically, these young heartworms take two to three months to move through the body and take up residence in the heart and pulmonary arteries, where they grow into adulthood in three months. Adult heartworms can survive in a dog for five to seven years. In addition to causing heart failure, heartworms may damage to the liver and kidneys and other organs.

Though heartworm has been viewed as a threat only in mosquito season, largely confined to the Southeast and Mississippi River Valley, the reality is that every state now reports it. What's more, with owners increasingly traveling with their dogs, more are exposed throughout the year.

Despite the availability of preventatives—the latest an injectable offering six months of protection—the number of cases of heartworm infection has remained the same for the past decade. That was one of the surprising findings in a Gallup survey of eighteen thousand veterinary clinics. Veterinarians diagnosed nearly a quarter million cats and dogs with the disease in 2001, the survey found.

One possible reason: the use of preventatives in dog-owning households in the United States fell from 66 percent in 1998 to 55 percent in 2001, according to the survey, sponsored by the American Heartworm Society and Merial, a maker of preventatives.

The finding underscores the need for owner education, sponsors said. Some owners forget to give preventatives regularly. Others mistakenly believe their indoor dog won't become infected. In fact, the tiny female mosquitoes that transmit the disease can easily slip through screens and openings around doors and windows. And even quick outdoor trips for elimination expose a dog to mosquitoes.

"Heartworm also continues to be a threat because the disease lives in stray dogs," says Michael Stone, a veterinary internist and assistant clinical professor at Tufts. "When a mosquito bites an infected pet, the mosquito becomes contagious to neighboring pets. Although mosquitoes tend to fly less than a quarter mile, they can travel farther with a strong breeze."

Every State Reports Heartworm Disease

At least 250,000 dogs and cats tested positive for heartworm in a 2001 survey of veterinary clinics nationwide, according to the American Heartworm Society and Merial, a maker of Heartguard brand products.

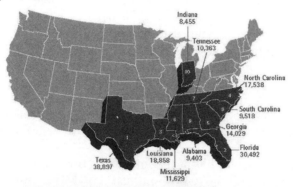

Healthy heart

Infected heart

State	Number of Positive Tests in Dogs	Number of Positive Tests in Cats	Percent of State's Clinics Reporting
1. Texas	38,535	362	64 percent
2. Florida	29,749	743	78 percent
3. Louisiana	18,700	158	74 percent
4. North Carolina	17,338	200	78 percent
5. Georgia	13,896	133	64 percent
6. Mississippi	11,522	107	73 percent
7. Tennessee	10,324	39	92 percent
8. South Carolina	9,387	131	78 percent
9. Alabama	9,308	95	83 percent
10. Indiana	8,348	107	73 percent

The survey involved 25,000 veterinary clinics, of which nearly 18,000 responded; 244,291 cases of heartworm in dogs were reported by the responding clinics.

The Signs

Infected dogs exhibit few symptoms. They may be somewhat lethargic and cough and show a loss of appetite and intolerance for exercise. More severely affected dogs will suffer shortness of breath, pronounced weight loss, weakness, listlessness, fainting, fever, and— if the disease is well advanced—collapse and death. Some dogs show no signs of heartworm for up to two years. When they do, they're in the advanced stages, facing costly, sometimes risky, treatment and complications, and a recovery process that can take months.

The most effective way to determine if your dog has heartworm disease is via a blood test in which your veterinarian can determine whether microfilariae are in the canine's bloodstream.

The Treatment

If your veterinarian determines your dog has heartworm disease, he or she is most likely to give the animal a series of injections called adulticide to wipe out the parasites. Complete rest is required after the treatment.

Veterinarians give two injections at a twenty-four-hour interval. Severely affected dogs receive a single initial injection followed in one month by two injections at a twenty-four-hour interval.

One of the risks of adulticides is that dying worms can block blood flow. "The most serious complications of heartworm therapy occur two to three weeks after adulticide administration," Dr. Stone says. "Acute lung injury occurs in response to dying heartworms. There is also a significant immunological response to the dying worm fragments. Strict exercise restriction and low cardiac output are important to facilitate lung repair."

Owners must crate their dog and allow only brief trips outdoors to eliminate for at least one month. Many dogs will have a mild cough during this time, which is not cause for concern, but shortness of breath should be considered an emergency, Dr. Stone says. "Oxygen therapy, glucocorticoids and absolute confinement with or without careful intravenous fluid therapy are necessary."

Four to six weeks after the giving the adulticide, veterinarians administer a drug to kill the microfilaria. They keep the patient at the hospital for eight hours after treatment and watch for signs of weakness, lethargy, abnormally fast heartbeat and shock. If a test for microfilaria two weeks later is negative, they'll begin preventive therapy.

It's far easier to prevent the disease in the first place. Your veterinarian first will run a blood test to make sure your dog is not currently infected. If the test comes back negatively, he or she will recommend a preventative such as a periodic injection, a topical treatment, or tablet. Owners can begin giving preventatives to dogs as young as six to eight weeks, Dr. Stone says.

Controversy exists as to the best way to protect the greatest number of pets. "The usual recommendation has been to administer preventives in the June-to-November mosquito season in the southern third of the U.S.," Dr. Stone says. "However, year-round monthly preventive therapy is often considered prudent. Additional benefits, including control of internal parasites and fleas, may justify year-round administration in other climates. Another consideration is the 'oops-I-forgot' factor, when owners are less likely to forget medication if it's given every month as opposed to only certain times of the year."

Daily dosing with dieithycarbabamazine, or DEC, has fallen out of favor, its popularity overtaken by monthly medications, Dr. Stone says. "It's also inconvenient because, if as few as three doses are missed, the animal may catch heartworm. Monthly products are very popular, with some having additional benefits, such as control of internal and external parasites. A six-month injection has recently become available for dogs; however, the injection does not provide continuous control of internal and external parasites."

Consult with your veterinarian about the method most appropriate for you and your dog. And remember: heartworm disease is almost 100 percent preventable as long as owners take appropriate measures.

Mites

Mites—those eight-legged microscopic pests—can wreak havoc with dogs. Ear mites seem to primarily be a problem for puppies, while puppies and dogs can be the victims of mange, caused by one of three types of mites. Fortunately, the conditions are treatable.

Dr. Nesbitt outlined the three most common types of mange:

■ Demodectic mange, also called red mange and canine demodicosis after the mite Demodex canis. Demodex mites exist throughout the country. They're contracted from the mother while nursing in the first two to three days of life. The mites take up residence in skin pores. They sip sebum and produce a substance that lowers a dog's resistance to them. The dog's body often resists the mite, but sometimes a change—genetic predisposition to the generalized form and physical stress play roles—lowers that resistance, triggering out-of-control mite multiplication.

■ Cheyletiella mange, or walking dandruff, which most often affects puppies.

■ Sarcoptic mange, or scabies, which most frequently involves the edges of earflaps, the outside of elbows, and hocks. Dogs who are outdoors a lot tend to contract Sarcoptes scabiei canis mites more often. If your dog goes untreated, female Sarcoptes mites will burrow under the upper layer of skin, thrive and create offspring.

No breed seems immune from mite invasions, though at least 26 breeds may be genetically predisposed to immunity conditions favoring the lifestyle of Demodex canis.

The Signs

With ear mites, itchiness is the primary symptom. The scratching may be so severe that your dog develops bleeding sores. Excessive head shaking is another symptom, and a discharge from the ears is common.

With demodectic mange, the mite infestation may be localized or generalized. It may begin as a localized condition and spread. The generalized form is associated with an immune deficiency. As mites and debris clog the victim's hair follicles, the dog may lose hair in patches. Staphylococcus infection may move in, causing the skin to become inflamed and ooze. "It's not itchy unless there's a secondary infection," Dr. Nesbitt says.

Conversely, he says an acute onset of intense itching characterizes sarcoptic mange. The dog's fierce scratching can lead to secondary bacterial skin infections.

Cheyletiella mange differs from the others in that the itching it causes is mild, but the mites cause a dusting of dandruff on the head, neck and back.

All manges may mimic other skin conditions, such as flea allergies and airborne allergies, or atopy, making it nearly impossible for a dog owner to diagnose the problem. Allergy and mange may occur concurrently.

"Skin scrapings are the way to identify any of the mites," Dr. Nesbitt says. The scrapings lift mites, 1/60 to 1/250 of an inch long, from their hiding places—ear mites in the ears, demodex in hair follicles, cheyletiella from the skin surface, and Sarcoptes in the top layers of skin. Veterinarians then identify them positively under a microscope.

The Treatment

Especially if the infestation is severe, it is important to consult with your veterinarian on an action plan to see that the mites are eradicated.

Ear mite treatment generally involves a thorough cleaning as well as medication. For Demodex mites, your veterinarian may prescribe amitraz dips or Ivermectin. Ivermectin can't be given to Collies, Shetland Sheepdogs or other herding breeds; it's toxic to them. Sarcoptes mites also succumb to Ivermectin and selamectin. Cheyletiella mites are fought with Ivermectin, fipronil, lime sulfur dips, or topical flea products.

Treatment for sarcoptic mange lasts three to four weeks. Generalized demodectic mange is the most stubborn, requiring three to six months of treatment; the localized form may go away spontaneously.

Once cured, a dog can get mange again, though recurrence of sarcoptic mange is uncommon; most dogs who have it develop an immunity to it.

Spiders

Only two species of spiders in the United States are known to have caused serious diseases and reports of death, and the latter are rare. They are the black widow and brown recluse spiders.

The female black widow spider carries enough neurotoxin venom to injure or kill a small dog. The black widow is a half-inch to an inch across and typically is shiny black. Five species of black widows are found in the United States; the spiders generally are found in southern and western states, though they are found in every state except Alaska. They usually are found in their webs in protected areas, such as the corners of doors and windows, or in littered areas.

The brown recluse spider is a half-inch to two inches long with a fiddle-shaped mark on its back. The spider is found almost exclusively in the Southeast and Midwest.

The Signs

A dog who has been bitten by a black widow spider will be in pain around his or her mouth and may experience nausea, swelling, muscle tremors, rigid muscles, paralysis, difficulty in breathing, and spasms. Onset of the signs may take two or more hours. Death usually is the result of paralysis of muscles associated with breathing.

A bite by a brown recluse spider typically will result in lethargy, vomiting, bleeding and an enlarging wound. The bite doesn't cause much pain, but a reddened area develops and underlying tissue may die.

The Treatment

If your dog is bitten by a black widow spider, take the animal to a veterinarian immediately. The veterinarian can administer muscle relaxants to ease the symptoms.

A wound caused by a brown recluse spider's bite may heal on its own in several weeks. but a veterinarian can provide antibiotics to stop infection. Surgery may be needed to remove dead skin and tissue.

Scorpions

They sting with a venom containing a digestive enzyme fatal to bugs, their main food. Not all are deadly to larger creatures. However, the venom of the bark scorpion—found primarily in Arizona and in smaller populations in parts of California and Utah—also contains venom toxic to the nervous system. The sting's effect varies with the dog's size, but all stung dogs need immediate veterinary attention.

The Signs
Symptoms may begin an hour after the sting and may include drooling, teary eyes, frequent urination and defecation, dilated pupils, muscle tremors, breathing difficulty and collapse. The symptoms may be mistaken for epilepsy or exposure to pesticides.

The Treatment
If the stinger remains in the skin, the owner or veterinarian can remove it carefully. Treatment includes intravenous fluids and pain relief. If signs of toxicity worsen, the veterinarian may reduce tremors and control seizures with medication. No blood test exists to positively identify scorpion venom.

Wasps and Bees

Many dogs suffer wasp and bee stings, but most treatments can be advised by phone. "Most stings occur on the head and paws, probably because of a dog's nosy nature," says Tufts' Dr. Stone.

The Signs
Stung dogs typically experience mild redness, swelling, and pain around the affected area. Allergic reactions, though rare, include swelling, vomiting, excessive urination and defecation, muscle weakness, and seizures.

The Treatment
Ice compresses may reduce swelling and pain. Large, local swelling such as the swelling of a leg or the face should be monitored in a veterinary hospital, Dr. Stone says. Attacks by swarms of bees require immediate veterinary attention.

The Best Advice

Stings and bites of all sorts can be difficult to find in a dog's haircoat, but any unusual symptoms or behavior may signal their presence. Insect and arachnid stings and bites can be an annoyance or life threatening. In every case, an ounce of prevention can be worth a pound of cure. ■

5

Aging Dogs

*Help your dog make the most of
his or her golden years.*

First, you might notice a few white hairs on your dog's muzzle, or maybe a bluish cast over the eyes. Or maybe your pet isn't as up for a long walk as he or she was a few months ago. Maybe he or she is spending more and more time alone, away from the family pack. Then it dawns on you that that lovable puppy has become a senior citizen.

The point at which a dog qualifies as "aged" varies. Veterinarians generally consider small dogs to be senior citizens at about twelve years old while large dogs reach the senior stage at six to ten years. This roughly corresponds to the fifty-five-plus category in people. National surveys indicate more than 18 million dogs are at least seven years old.

The good news is that you and your aging dog may have many more years together. Medical advances are providing new ways to deal with issues such as canine cognitive dysfunction, which is somewhat similar to the confusion experienced by humans who suffer from Alzheimer's disease.

Still, it's important to recognize that aging dogs may experience health problems that are uncommon in younger dogs, including diabetes mellitus; kidney, heart, and liver disease; hormonal anomalies such as Cushing's disease; periodontal disease; arthritis; and cancer. Owners of older dogs should look out for any signs of pain; changes in body weight; variations in digestion and elimination habits; joint stiffness; skin and mouth growths; and decreased in-

How Old Is Your Dog In Human Years?

Generally, big dogs age faster than small ones. Use this chart to determine if your dog is in his adult prime or geriatric. For example, a 6-year-old dog weighing less than 20 pounds is the equivalent of a 40-year-old person, but a 6-year-old dog weighing more than 120 pounds is the equivalent of a 69-year-old.

William Fortney, DVM, a veterinarian specializing in geriatric medicine and director of community care at Kansas State University School of Veterinary Medicine in Manhattan, Kan., devised the chart.

| | WEIGHT (IN POUNDS) | | | |
	0-20	21-50	51-120	120+
3 yrs.	28	29	31	39
4 yrs.	32	34	38	49
5 yrs.	36	39	45	59
6 yrs.	40	44	52	69
7 yrs.	44	49	59	79
8 yrs.	48	54	66	89
9 yrs.	52	59	73	99
10 yrs.	56	64	80	—
11 yrs.	60	69	87	—
12 yrs.	64	74	94	—
13 yrs.	68	79	—	—
14 yrs.	72	84	—	—
15 yrs.	76	89	—	—
16 yrs.	80	94	—	—
17 yrs.	84	—	—	—
18 yrs.	88	—	—	—
19 yrs.	92	—	—	—
20 yrs.	96	—	—	—

AGE IN ACTUAL YEARS

teraction with people and the environment.

To catch age-related disorders at the earliest possible stage, veterinarians often perform disease-screening blood tests during annual checkups for older dogs. A yearly examination is roughly equivalent to a person seeing a physician every five years; some veterinarians now recommend biannual visits.

Cognitive Dysfunction Syndrome

Age-related cognitive impairment is becoming more recognized in veterinary medicine. Recent studies indicate 25 percent of dogs one to twelve years of age show some signs of cognitive impairment related to orientation in the home or yard, social interaction, house-

Owners should be sure older dogs always have a supply of fresh water.

training or the sleep/wake cycle. The percentage of fifteen- to sixteen-year-old dogs with signs of cognitive impairment increases to almost 70 percent, says Raymond Kudej, veterinary surgeon at Tufts University School of Veterinary Medicine. Older animals with this impairment may pace or vocalize at night, and sleep less during the day.

The exact cause of age-related cognitive impairment is unknown. "Currently, we ... must rule out other conditions through physical assessment, MRIs and CT scans and blood tests to tell us that a dog may have CDS," says Dominik Faissler, veterinary neurologist at Tufts. "I always encourage people to seek professional help for their older dogs if their dogs are displaying strange behaviors because treatments are now available that won't cure age-related dysfunction but can at least slow down the degenerative process."

The DISH Syndrome

Older dogs with memory loss may display what experts describe as the DISH acronym for cognitive dysfunction syndrome.

■ **Disorientation.** Note if your dog wanders aimlessly, becomes lost in your house or stares blankly at walls.

■ **Interaction reduction.** Alert the veterinarian if your dog seems to forget his or her name, fails to greet you when you come home, or walks away from you in a confused way in the middle of receiving affection.

■ **Sleep difficulties.** Have you noticed your dog now wakes up in the middle of the night and howls or barks for no reason? Or, is the animal sleeping more during the day?

■ **House soiling.** Report any incidents of your dog urinating or defecating in your home minutes after being outside. Don't forgo seeking help from veterinarians until the soiling becomes intolerable. By then, it may be too late for medical or surgical intervention.

Dealing With CDS

New medications, behavior modifications, and nutrition are your best weapons to combat the effects of aging, Dr. Faissler says. He treats many older dogs with Anipryl (selegiline hydrochloride), a memory-improving medication manufactured by Pfizer that received Food and Drug Administration approval in late 1998.

"Anipryl changes the neurotransmitters in the brain to help dogs function better and interact better with their owners," Dr. Faissler says. However, not all dogs who are given Anipryl see significant improvements.

Cushing's Disease

Middle-aged to older dogs also are more prone to Cushing's disease. Cushing's occurs in slightly more females than males, but because its symptoms—constant panting, frequent urination, ravenous appetite, hair loss and muscle weakness—can mimic those of aging, it often goes undetected and untreated. Beagles, Boston Terriers, Boxers, Dachshunds, Miniature and Toy Poodles, German Shepherds, Golden Retrievers, and Yorkshire Terriers are the breeds most often affected.

"As long as an owner works with veterinarian and is aware of the clinical signs to watch for, dogs with Cushing's can regain their normal activities," says Linda Ross, a Tufts associate professor of internal medicine.

Cushing's disease (hyperadrenocorticism) is one of the most common hormonal diseases found in dogs more than ten years of age. It occurs when too much cortisone is in the body. This develops most commonly when the adrenal glands produce too much cortisol. The hormone cortisol is responsible for maintaining a normal blood glucose level, facilitates metabolism of fat, and supports the vascular and nervous systems. When too much is produced, it will affect all of the supporting systems of the body—the skeletal muscles, red blood cell production, immune system and kidneys. While dogs exhibit external signs of Cushing's that owners and veterinarians can see, they also have damage to the liver, kidneys, and heart.

Located adjacent to the kidneys, the two tiny adrenal glands secrete vital hormones under the control of the pituitary gland in the brain.

Excessive hormone secretion can be caused by underlying abnormal or benign tumors in the pituitary gland or from benign or malignant tumors within the adrenal glands themselves. More than 80 to 85 percent of dogs with Cushing's have the pituitary-dependent hyperadrenocorticism (PDH) form of the disease.

With the pituitary-dependent form of Cushing's, many veterinarians prescribe Lysodren (mitotane). It destroys the outer layer of the adrenal glands, which limits their ability to produce cortisol in response to signals from the hyperactive pituitary gland. Initially, there is an induction phase when the medication is given, and the dog is given Lysodren every day for seven to fourteen days. This is followed by a maintenance dose given once a week. Owners must carefully monitor the amount of food and water a dog takes as well as the animal's overall disposition. This helps them recognize when the drug is taking effect because symptoms will abate.

Veterinarians recommend the dogs have follow-up blood tests, a urinalysis and ACTH suppression tests every three to four months. The cost of identifying, treating and monitoring a dog with Cushing's can range from several hundred dollars to several thousand, depending upon the severity of the case and the number of tests required.

Some veterinarians prescribe Anipryl, which is newer than Lysodren. Used to treat Parkinson's disease in people and cognitive dysfunction in dogs, it's thought Anipryl may alleviate the clinical signs of Cushing's by restoring the natural balance of important brain chemicals, especially dopamine.

However, "many veterinarians are cautious about prescribing it for treatment of Cushing's disease," Dr. Ross says. "Studies have not shown that it actually changes the levels of cortisone or the levels of ACTH in a dog with Cushing's; clinical signs improve in only about 20 percent of cases." Anipryl is metabolized to amphetamine and would not be recommended in a dog who also had heart or kidney disease.

Cushing's may cause serious complications—urinary tract infections, pulmonary embolisms (sudden blockage of an artery by a blood clot) and blindness, but the majority of dogs with it die from the effects of old age, such as kidney or heart failure.

Food

Pet-food companies have created an unofficial arbitrary "senior" life stage for dogs, but "we don't know for certain what older dogs as a group need nutritionally," says Lisa Freeman, associate professor and veterinary nutritionist at Tufts University School of Veterinary Medicine. "So there's no reason to automatically switch a healthy seven- or eight-year-old dog to a so-called 'senior' diet."

Because senior dogs sometimes are less active, some do experience weight gains; however, others lose weight because disease, pain, or just plain forgetfulness cause them to eat less. In either case, it's important to keep your dog at his or her ideal weight. If your dog has a significant weight gain or loss, be sure to consult your vet.

"When it comes to nutrition, treating older dogs as individuals is extremely important," Dr. Freeman says.

Lumps

Lumps and bumps are found in a variety of places on a dog's body and are not necessarily cause for excessive concern. Lipomas, fatty tumors found under the skin, are most common in middle-aged or older dogs, and overweight female dogs are particularly prone to them. Once a dog gets one lipoma, more are likely to follow.

These soft, rounded lumps aren't painful to the dog if touched. Most often they're found underneath the skin, but they occasionally can be found deeper in the body, where they pose little threat to health.

Doberman Pinschers, Miniature Schnauzers, and Labrador Retrievers, in addition to mixed breeds, seem to have a genetic predisposition to develop lipomas.

"In dogs, probably 90 percent of skin lumps are benign," says John Berg, veterinary surgeon and chair of Tufts' Department of Clinical Sciences. "They don't even need to be removed. Some dogs are genetically predisposed to bumps, and can have ten to twenty of them, all benign."

Benign growths stay in place and don't metastasize, or spread; however, they can grow to significant size, large enough that they can interfere with the dog's movement or functions.

"Owners should periodically look all over and feel all over the dog to check for lumps," Dr. Berg says. "It's amazing how large and advanced they can get in hidden places like under the armpit, and it can be difficult to treat them if they get huge. If owners find a new lump, they shouldn't ignore it. See your veterinarian. Wait and see might be the best approach, but ask your veterinarian if that is appropriate for a certain lump."

If your veterinarian sees no reason to treat the lump, check it periodically to see if it grows bigger or changes in any way. Dr. Berg discourages removal of multiple lumps solely for the sake of appearance: "Cosmetics is not a good reason."

Your veterinarian may suggest that a lump be aspirated, a procedure that allows cells from the lump to be examined in a laboratory. No sedation or anesthesia is necessary as a needle is inserted into the lump and a plunger withdraws some cells through suction. It's not a painful procedure. Most dogs don't even notice that it's happening. Veterinarians examine the cells under a microscope, and the results can be had within minutes.

A needle aspirate usually will indicate if the lump is benign. The main purpose of a needle aspirate is to rule out a mast cell—a connective tissue cell—tumor.

If the lump is benign, there's no need to remove it unless it impedes the dog's comfort because of its location or threatens to become difficult to remove if it continues to grow. However, the veterinarian will instruct the owner to want for any changes in it.

A biopsy is a more involved, accurate procedure. Tissue is collected for examination under a microscope. A biopsy requires general anesthesia or at least heavy sedation, and it takes two to four days for the results to be processed. "The biopsy is the gold standard for determining what's going on," Dr. Berg says. "Owners should not fear that a biopsy or aspirate will make a lump become or behave worse. If your veterinarian recommends it, feel comfortable going forward with it as it's a standard workup test."

The best way to check for lumps and bumps is to regularly run your hands over the dog's entire body. If your dog goes to a groomer, the groomer may find a growth and tell you. But if you groom, brush, and pet your dog, that's the perfect time to check him or her out.

The dog will think he or she is being loved, but you'll know that you're providing both a health check and a bonding experience—a true win-win situation.

Tips for Keeping Your Older Dog Healthy

*The Senior Dogs Project promotes adoption of older dogs, provides current information on older dogs' special care needs, and documents the strong, loving bonds that people have with their older dogs. These tips from the project's Web site, **www.srdogs.com**, are reprinted here with permission.*

1. Establish a relationship with the best veterinarian you can find. For most older dogs, it is advisable to make an appointment with the vet every six months. Your vet should be someone whom you trust and with whom you feel very comfortable.

2. Become informed about the conditions common to older dogs and the therapies used for them. Be alert to symptoms, bring them to your vet's attention promptly, and be prepared to discuss treatment options.

3. Feed your older dog the best food you can afford; consider feeding him or her a home-prepared diet and two small meals daily rather than one large one.

4. Don't overfeed your dog. Obesity will create health problems and shorten his or her life.

5. Consider the use of dietary supplements such as glucosamine/chondroitin for arthritis.

6. Give your senior dog adequate exercise, but adjust it to his or her changing abilities.

7. Attend to your dog's dental health. Brush the teeth daily and have them cleaned professionally whenever your vet advises it.

8. Tell your vet you wish to have your dog vaccinated only once every three years, as currently advised by some major veterinary colleges.

9. Be diligent in controlling fleas and ticks, and keep your dog and his or her environment scrupulously clean.

10. Make your senior dog as much a part of your life as possible, and do all you can to keep the animal interested, active, happy, and comfortable.

Keeping Your Dog Engaged

Owners can take greater responsibilities in helping slow the aging process by noting early changes in their dogs' appetites, behaviors and physical conditions. Veterinarians offer these recommendations:

■ **Reinforce basic commands.** You can teach an aging dog to "Sit" before heading out the door for a walk or "Give me a paw" shake before setting down his or her food bowl. Test hearing and sight by

Your dog may suffer from canine cognitive dysfunction if he or she becomes less engaged with the rest of your famliy pack.

teaching your dog to make eye contact with you and then incorporate hand signal commands.

■ **Play mental gymnastic games.** Keep your dog mentally stimulated by playing a game of hide and seek with food treats stashed in different rooms of the house. Or serve your dog food puzzles, such as peanut butter-filled Kong toys or kibble-filled cubes.

■ **Stick with short walks.** Take your aging dog for shorter but more frequent walks on soft surfaces that won't jar the joints. Vary the routes to expose your dog to new sights, sounds, and smells.

■ **Encourage your dog to stretch.** Prior to play time or walks, have your dog get into a "play bow" position—head down, front legs low and stretched forward, and back end up. This natural full-body stretch helps improve circulation and warm the muscles. After a walk or activity, gently stretch your dog's legs and massage the torso.

■ **Add more water bowls.** As dogs age, they tend to drink less and run the risk of dehydration. Put a few more water bowls inside your home and measure the water in the morning and at night to make sure your dog drinks enough water. Wipe up spills so that your dog doesn't slip and get injured.

Twice a Year for Life

The American Veterinary Medicine Association recommends that senior dogs see the veterinarian every six months. The group's national publicity campaign supporting that recommendation is themed, "Twice a Year for Life."

With a third of American households owning a dog and/or cat, the nation's veterinarians want pet owners to know more about their pets' aging process and its impact on health and quality of life.

"Advances in veterinary medicine have led to an increased percentage of aging cats and dogs in this country," says former AVMA President Jack O. Walther. "Unlike people, cats and dogs can't tell you where it hurts. An examination every six months is the best way to ensure that any potentially life-threatening condition is caught early."

Because dogs age faster than people do, significant health changes can occur in as little as three to six months, Walther says. "An exam every six months provides the opportunity for early detection, treatment, or prevention of potentially life-threatening conditions."

The AVMA recommends that in addition to other tests, dogs over the age of seven undergo an osteoarthritis check, thoracic radiographic exam, and screen for hypothyroidism every six months. ■

6

Preventing "Lost Dog"

*One of the kindest things you can
do for your dog is provide him or her
with proper identification.*

We go to great lengths to ensure our dogs' safety. We leash them, fence them, keep them indoors or close to our sides. Yet accidents happen. A door doesn't close tightly. The meter reader leaves the gate open. A section of fence falls down in a windstorm, flood, or earthquake. We're in a car accident and our dog panics, jumps through the broken windshield, and runs off. While safe, appropriate confinement is a critical first-line defense against pet loss, proper identification is your lost dog's "ticket" home when the first line fails. It's one of the most caring things you can do for your dog, and one of the first things you should do when you acquire your new pet.

No animal shelter monitoring organization tracks national statistics about lost pets, but of the eight to ten million animals coming into shelters every year, only 15 to 30 percent of dogs are reclaimed, according to Betsy McFarland, program director for animal sheltering issues at the Humane Society of the United States (HSUS) in Washington, D.C. "You may be the best dog owner on the planet, but if someone leaves your gate open, it can happen," she says.

The American Society for the Prevention of Cruelty to Animals (ASPCA) estimates that about half the animals taken in by shelters are relinquished by their owners, and the other half are picked up by animal control.

Proactive recovery efforts can determine whether you'll recover

Even the best fence is only as good as the people who remember to close it.

your dog—or if you will find yourself in the terrible, heartbreaking position of never knowing what happened to your missing dog.

An Ounce of Prevention

Obviously, preventing pet loss in the first place is ideal. While you can't plan for every possible scenario, you can increase the odds of keeping your pet safe with these commonsense strategies:

■ **Keep your dog secure in a fenced yard or on a leash.** "I think the most common reason people lose their dogs is because they let them outside, off lead and unsupervised for prolonged periods. It doesn't take much distraction for loose dogs to catch a scent or see something interesting, and off they go," said Mary Labato, veterinary internist at Tufts University School of Veterinary Medicine. Fences should be tall, deep and secure enough to prevent escape. Use a leash on outings. Pens work for some dogs, but Dr. Labato advises against tie-outs: "Dogs can tangle themselves in the tie and injury, such as choking or limb lacerations, can occur."

■ **Don't leave your dog unsupervised.** Supervision entails more than a secure fence. It means not leaving your dog outside for long periods while you're away and not leaving your dog unsupervised in the car. A bored dog may find ways to escape.

■ **Have your dog spayed or neutered.** According to the ASPCA, 75 percent of pets are spayed or neutered, but only 10 percent of animals coming into shelters have been. A spayed/neutered dog is less likely to roam.

■ **Obedience-train your dog.** Dogs who have had formal obedience training are much less likely to end up in shelters, according to the HSUS. Obedience-trained dogs are more likely to stop when told rather than bolt out a front door, car, or otherwise out of sight.

■ **Keep good records and a photograph.** Keep basic statistics about your pet easily accessible, including vaccination records and a color photo to use on posters and show neighbors, shelter workers, police and rescue groups. Knowing where to find this information instantly will save precious time if your dog goes missing.

■ **Take a DNA fingerprint.** Many purebred dog breeders already have records of their dogs' DNA profile for showing and breeding. This newer technology can establish identity and ownership beyond a doubt. "Your pet's DNA 'fingerprint' is a permanent, tamper-proof record of your pet's identity that is every bit as conclusive as the DNA evidence that can positively link a suspect to a crime or exonerate him," says Patricia Sapia, co-author of *The Complete Guide to Lost Pet Prevention & Recovery* (El Jebel Press). "Similarly, a DNA profile of your pet can win you a victory in court if your pet is ever lost and claimed by someone refusing to return the animal."

The American Kennel Club encourages and actively promotes the use of permanent DNA identification. Ask your veterinarian about DNA fingerprinting, or check the American Kennel Club Web site for more information at **www.akc.org/registration/dna**.

Which Kind of Identification?

Beyond prevention, thorough records and identification are the most effective ways to help the successful recovery of a lost dog. There are three primary types for dogs: ID tags, tattooing, and microchips. Each has its advantages and disadvantages. Keep in mind that whatever method or methods you choose, you must make the effort before your dog goes missing.

"We recommend using all three methods," says Kat Brown, director of operations for the Santa Cruz, Calif., SPCA. "A regular ID tag is most helpful for the finder. A chip is great backup when you have shelters and vets in your area that scan. A tattoo is triple insurance." In other words, why not give your dog two or three "tickets" home?

ID Tags

Most people who find a dog will promptly contact the owner and return the dog home if they can. A simple identification tag with your phone number—and, if you are comfortable with it, your address—makes it easy for someone picking up your pet to phone and reunite you. Rabies tags and license tags also contain identifying information.

An ID tag gives the finder immediate information and facilitates a speedy reunion, saving a trip to the nearest animal shelter and hours or days of anxious searching by the owner. A license can do the same after one quick call to animal control to get owner information. Many animal control agencies also have a policy of trying to return a dog home if the animal is wearing a current license or ID rather than resorting to impounding the dog.

"A lot of people feel like licensing of the animal is just another tax, and if they have a nice name tag, that's good enough," says Stacey Candella, director of Pets 911, an online clearinghouse. "But you would be surprised at how many animals lose some of their tags. If you have a tag from the county, that means the animal is in the system, and it will have all your information."

Identification tags come in numerous forms—metal, plastic, instant, mail-order, cute, and utilitarian. It doesn't matter which you use, as long as you have one on your dogs at all times.

Because tags provide potential for the quickest trip home for your dog, most shelter officials strongly urge that dogs wear ID tags and licenses at all times, even when the dog is safe at home.

There are a wide variety of ID tags, and it probably doesn't matter which you use as long as you use one of them. Temporary paper-and-plastic tags can be filled out with a permanent marker and then sealed, allowing for instant security. You can send away for fancy engraved tags that will never fade or suffer water damage. There are even "talking" ID tags that play a recorded message to your dog's rescuer.

Make your choice based on your and your dog's needs—immediacy, durability, and fashion statement—and then consider the added protection of backup methods of ID, because the ID tag is not the perfect solution. Tags and collars can fall off or can be removed by unfriendly people.

Some owners don't like to use tags, citing the annoyance of the jingling of tags as the dog moves around or scratches at an errant flea. While the annoyance seems minor in comparison to the trauma of losing a dog, an easy solution to this complaint is to tape or rivet the tags flat against the collar, or to buy a flat leather collar to which a flat ID tag is riveted.

Tattoos

Tattooing takes the collar ID concept one step further, by giving the dog a form of unremovable (and silent!) identification. It involves the injection of ink under the dog's skin with an electronic pen. When the tattoo technician "writes" with the pen, a tiny needle injects the ink to a depth of $\frac{1}{32}$ of an inch under the skin, in a series of numbers or letters. Dogs may or may not be anesthetized during the procedure, which can run from twenty to more than one hundred dollars. The procedure is touted as being quick and painless.

Tattoos are usually placed on the bare skin inside a dog's flank, or sometimes, as in the case of racing greyhounds, in the dog's ear. Tattoos cannot be lost or removed, and they are pretty durable, although an unscrupulous person can alter a tattoo. Tattoos can be a great way to prove ownership in a custody or identity dispute.

The tattoo dilemma has to do with what you choose to write. In today's transient society, a phone number is no good; a person might move several times in the dog's life, and area codes can change. Some owners tattoo their pets with their Social Security number (SSN) or driver's license number, but these, too, are problematic.

For security reasons, neither Social Security Administration nor state driver's licensing officials will release a person's address or phone number. Local police departments and city animal shelters which are affiliated with the local police departments can access driver's license information and contact the owners, but they cannot trace Social Security numbers.

Registration companies facilitate tattoo tracing, but finding an owner can still be a frustrating proposition, since not all owners register their dogs' tattoos with one of or both of these two groups. Tufts' Dr. Labato also notes that the tattoo registry system is less extensive than the one for microchips.

If you have a purebred dog, the American Kennel Club recommends tattooing it with its AKC registration number. The Club has established a unit, the Companion Animal Recovery, that will assist owners in becoming reunited with their dogs.

A final frustration is that most shelters don't routinely roll incoming dogs onto their backs to look for tattoos. Many dogs don't take kindly to being rolled on their backs by a stranger, especially in the high-stress environment of an animal shelter, and shelters are understandably reluctant to risk bites to staff from dogs who protest the procedure. However, most shelters, but by no means all, will make an effort to look for tattoos immediately prior to euthanasia, if a dog will tolerate the search.

Microchipping

The third dog identification option is microchipping, also known as "radio frequency identification." The high-tech member of the dog ID team has been available commercially for companion animal identification since 1988.

The microchip is a tiny computer chip etched with an identification code. The chip is attached to an antenna and encased in surgical-grade glass to form a transponder, or tag. The transponder is about the size of a grain of rice, and when injected under the skin between a dog's shoulder blades, is unnoticeable on all but the smallest and most short-haired dogs. The injection process takes only a few seconds, requires no anesthesia, and is no more painful for a pet than a vaccination.

A special receiver is used to "read" the chip's transponder by use of a tiny radio frequency signal. Shelter staff scanning a lost pet can use the code to locate the owner of the animal, or to retrieve any other information stored in the system's database. The life expectancy of the chip is twenty to twenty-five years, and the cost of chipping is affordable to most pet owners—from fifteen dollars at

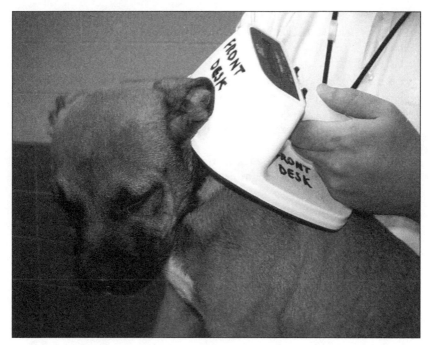

If your lost dog has been "chipped," many shelters can easily use a reader to help get him or her back home quickly.

some animal shelters to fifty dollars or more at veterinary hospitals, with an additional cost for lifetime registration in some system databases.

"Microchipping is so crucial," Candella says. "This little implant between your dog's shoulder blades identifies your dog, and the first thing many shelters and rescue groups do when they get in a dog is to scan for that microchip."

A permanent, unalterable method of pet identification sounds almost too good to be true, and of course, it is. It's important that you send your contact information to a registry and keep it current; otherwise, the chip is of no good to you or your dog. Further, the "Big Brother" aspect of microchipping makes some people uncomfortable.

As with the tattoo system, not all shelters scan for chips, so some chip companies offer a visible ID tag to alert finders that the pet is chipped. Of course, the tag can be lost or removed. It is also possible to miss a chip while scanning, although over the last decade the quality of scanners has improved. Fractious animals can be difficult to scan. Microchip manufacturers are working to invent newer, better technology.

Lost Dog Checklist

First

■ *Call local police, animal-control officer, and animal shelter(s). Even if the police won't look for your pet, a report establishes a record your dog was lost and can help later in identifying him or her or in investigating pet theft.*

■ *Call all tag, tattoo, or microchip registries with which you have registered your dog.*

■ *Alert your neighbors.*

■ *Mobilize friends to begin an immediate search.*

■ *Make sure your answering machine is on.*

■ *Leave the fence gate open so the animal can return on his or her own.*

■ *Place items with your scent in the dog's crate, and leave the crate where the dog was last seen.*

Next

■ *Call the state police or highway patrol, along with sheriffs, animal-control officers, police departments, and animal shelters in surrounding towns.*

■ *Notify all area emergency animal hospitals that you guarantee payment for treatment if your dog is found and brought in.*

■ *Keep a list of all people and organizations you contact, with phone numbers.*

■ *Create and distribute a flyer with all pertinent information, including a clear photograph of your dog and a reward offer.*

■ *Visit nearby animal shelters and humane shelters to look for your dog, and go back often. "You have to go down there every day. You can't expect a busy shelter to monitor all the incoming dogs for you," says Stacey Candella, director of Pets 911, an online clearinghouse. "If you go down every day, you don't run the risk of missing your pet, who could come in and be adopted back out or even put to sleep. Check them all. Don't overlook any place that accepts stray animals."*

Follow-up

■ *Produce a professional-looking poster. Post it and send a copy to everyone you called.*

■ *Place ads offering a reward in local papers; take advantage of local TV and radio lost-pet announcements if available.*

■ *Consult online national databases that seek to reunite lost pets and their owners.*

■ *Consider hiring a pet detective. Keep in mind that fees vary widely.*

■ *Monitor calls carefully. While most people mean well, a few are out for reward money and may not even have your dog.*

■ *Don't agree to send money to someone who says he or she will ship your dog home. If someone offers to return your dog to you, set the meeting for a populated, well-lighted area and don't go alone.*

■ *Keep in touch with everyone you contacted in the beginning.*

■ *Don't give up your search. "I encourage people not to give up hope," says Betsy McFarland, HSUS program director for animal sheltering issues. "It might take a while to get your pet back, but the sooner you start looking, the better your chances are. People have been reunited with their pets months after they've gone missing."*

■ *After you've found your dog, call all your contacts to let them know your canine friend is safe and sound. They'll appreciate it.*

If the Worst Occurs

Act quickly if your dog becomes lost. "Time is the most critical factor when it comes to recovering a lost pet. Most lost pets that are recovered, are recovered relatively quickly and in close proximity to where they went missing," says Sapia. She cites a Florida pet detective who claims that, in his experience, 89 percent of lost pets are recovered if their owners searched actively for them in the first twelve hours after loss.

A bit of advice before you embark on the step-by-step search instructions outlined below: be sure that your dog is indeed missing by thoroughly searching your home, property, and neighborhood. Sometimes a "lost" puppy is asleep in a closet or under a bed.

If your dog is gone, don't be afraid to cast a wide net. A search area of ten miles is not unrealistic. "It is imperative that people extend their search range. Dogs often travel quickly and cover more distance than expected," Dr. Labato says. "Good Samaritans may also transport an animal they find to a hospital quite a distance away."

Sapia urges that you take a calm and well organized approach. "Losing a pet can be a heart-wrenching, time-consuming and costly event, but being prepared is your first line of defense," she says. "Doing what you can to prevent pet loss and having a recovery plan will afford pet owners the best opportunity to bring their missing pet home safely."

Spreading the Word

A good "Lost Dog" poster can be the key to recovering a lost pet. Effective posters are large and easy to read. An 8- by 14-inch or 11- by 17-inch poster draws more attention than a smaller sign. Effective posters also include a color picture of the animal, because what's "brown" or "red" or "brindle" to the owner may be "tan" or "rust" or "mottled" to someone else.

Here's how to make the best possible posters:

■ *Offer a reward, but make it for an unspecified amount to deter those who want to see if the dog is worth more than the reward.*

- *Don't be stingy. A few people might see one of ten or twenty posters, but many more will see two hundred or three hundred posters that you hang in well-traveled locations.*

- *Hang color copies of your poster in visible spots. "Post wherever you can: grocery stores, veterinary hospitals, pet stores, animal shelters, any place that allows you to post for free," said Stacey Candella, director of Pets 911, an online clearinghouse. "The more posters, the better."*

The ID Answer?

The best approach to identification is to cover all the bases. Certainly, all pets should wear ID tags at all times, not just when they are out for a walk. But in the event that tags are lost or removed, a back-up tattoo and/or a microchip, especially if they are registered with one or more registries, can literally mean the difference between life and death for your missing pet. ■

7

Boarding Options

*If you need to travel without
your dog, it's best to check out all
the possibilities in advance.*

Maybe it's a long-awaited vacation to Tahiti, a convention in Chicago, or an unexpected trip to deal with a family emergency. Whatever your destination, one fact is certain: you must leave your dog behind. How can you assure he or she will have the best care? You have many options. Some may even provide your pet a vacation of his or her own.

Before you choose a pet hotel over a pet sitter, know the pros and cons of all available choices, and determine—well before you book your tickets—the best situation for your dog.

The Best-Case Scenario

In an ideal world, you'd have a close friend or relative willing to take on pet-care duties while you're gone. This can be an especially attractive arrangement for a cash-strapped owner.

"The perfect situation would be that a friend takes care of the dog, and the dog stays in its own house," says John Berg, chair of the Department of Clinical Sciences at Tufts University School of Veterinary Medicine. "The change in routine is minimal and the dog is in a familiar place."

But if you don't have a pal with time to spare, consider hiring a pet sitter. Services range from walking and playing with your dog to staying in your home overnight. A pet sitter might visit your dog

For many people, it wouldn't be a vacation if they couldn't take along their beloved dogs.

in the morning and evening for feeding, exercise and playtime, and also bring in your mail and water the plants.

"Today's pet owners consider their pets part of the family and are taking better and better care of them," says Ellen Price, public relations manager of Pet Sitters International (PSI), an industry group based in North Carolina. "Some pets adjust fine to a kennel situation, but there are many advantages to keeping a pet in familiar surroundings."

Dogs who stay in their own homes avoid the stress of a new environment. They retain their customary diet and exercise routine. "You have the peace of mind knowing your pet is in confident, capable hands," Price says.

How many visits are sufficient? Most dogs should be let out to relieve themselves at least twice a day while the owner is away, Dr. Berg says. "Three or four times would be ideal."

On average, PSI members charge thirteen dollars per visit for one pet, but fees vary by region and can add up quickly. For example, Fetch Pet Sitting in Berkeley, Calif., charges twenty dollars for a thirty-minute visit and forty-five dollars for an overnight stay. If you want a sitter in the house at night providing two outings a day for your dog, the total cost can be daunting.

Before hiring a pet sitter, make sure he or she is bonded and insured. Check references. Interview several candidates and let your dog meet them, so you can observe how they interact. Set up a preliminary meeting to work out details. And schedule some services before your absence—like a series of walks—to get your dog used to the sitter.

Also, consider your dog's temperament and routine when determining whether pet sitting is appropriate. If he or she is accustomed to having someone around most of the time, requires frequent or intense exercise, or suffers from serious separation anxiety, pet sitting might not be the answer.

"Dogs are communal animals," says Dr. Nicholas Dodman, director of the Behavior Clinic at Tufts. "I think that it's probably not the greatest idea to leave them alone most of the day."

Finding the Best Sitter

*You'll likely find plenty of ads for pet sitters in your local yellow pages, on local Web sites, at your veterinarian's office, at the dog park, and in community newspapers. You can also locate one through the Web sites of Pet Sitters International (**www.petsit.com**) or the National Association of Professional Pet Sitters (**www.petsitters. org**). Here are some questions to ask prospective sitters, according to PSI. A full list is at **www.petsit.com/ petowners/ standards.asp**.*

- *Are they bonded and insured?*

- *Do they have references?*

- *Do they have a written contract that specifies services and fees?*

- *Do they have a veterinarian on call?*

- *Do they have a contingency plan for pet care in case of inclement weather or personal illness?*

- *Do they visit your home prior to the first visit and get detailed information about your dog?*

Boarding in a Private Home

If your dog needs more attention than a pet sitter can provide, consider boarding the animal in a private home. Laura Wagner of Richmond, Calif., has been taking in dogs for twenty-two years. She limits the number of boarding dogs in her home to two or three at a time. She has two Chow mixes and a Rottweiler-Australian Cattle Dog mix of her own. "The presence of other dogs is calming," she says. "When the dogs are together, they quickly find their rung in the pack."

A typical day finds the pack eating breakfast together at about 7:30 a.m., then heading to her large, fenced yard for play. Later, she'll take them all to off-leash park for a three-hour romp and swim for those inclined to hop into the canals in the park. Back home, it's nap time, dinner around 5 p.m. and a well-earned night of sleep.

Wagner, like most in-home caretakers, requires a prescreening for potential boarders. All dogs must be neutered or spayed, and have full vaccinations. She'll turn down aggressive dogs and eschews what she called "nervous, little froufrou dogs" who might find a change of environment unsettling.

Home boarding isn't ideal for dogs suffering from separation anxiety. "I had one dog I took in over my better judgment," Wagner recalls. "I went to the store for fifteen minutes. When I got back, I found my curtains had been shredded, a window had been broken, and two remote controls had been destroyed."

Before you home-board, have your dog meet the caretaker and his or her dogs, if any, in a neutral location. Visit the home to make sure you're comfortable with arrangements there. Ask if the caretaker will accommodate special needs for exercise, diet, and medication. Verify that other dogs boarding with yours are vaccinated and have been evaluated for temperament. And discuss emergency procedures such as what veterinarian will be consulted and the back-up plan if the caretaker becomes ill or indisposed.

If the home has an exercise yard, make sure it's secure. Look for a high fence with no loose dirt near the perimeters. The yard's surface matters, says Dr. Berg. "I'd normally prefer a dirt or grass-covered surface to concrete, especially if the dog doesn't get a lot of chance to run around on concrete. It's a really rough surface and can be abrasive on the pads."

It's a wise idea to board your dog for a trial, overnight run before you leave for a trip. If the animal enjoys the experience, you'll rest easy the next time boarding is necessary.

Parting Needn't Be Sorrowful

No matter which option you choose, these tips will help make good-bye easier for you and your dog.

- *Take the animal to visit the boarding facility. Sign up for doggie day care or do a trial, one-night boarding. If you're using a pet sitter, have that person take the dog for a few walks so they can get acquainted.*

- *If the caretaker won't allow you to bring your own dog's food, prepare for dietary changes. Consider transitioning the animal to the food at home. The kennel may provide you with a small supply. Otherwise, your dog will be at risk for gastrointestinal upset.*

- *Adapt nighttime habits. If your dog is used to sharing your bed, teach him or her to sleep on a dog bed as an alternative. This can help the animal adapt to sleeping alone in a kennel.*

- *Get your paperwork in order. Make sure you provide the caretaker with proof of vaccination, names and phone numbers of your veterinarian and emergency contacts, names and dosages of medications and any special instructions.*

- *When it's time to leave your dog, avoid prolonged, emotional farewells. Make your leaving low key or even fun—give your pet treats and praise and then quietly leave in the middle of the feel-good routine.*

- *Stage a quiet homecoming. Be calm and don't overexcite your dog in your joy over the reunion. The American Boarding Kennels Association recommends withholding food or water for four hours after homecoming to avoid stomach upset. If the dog is thirsty, place a few ice cubes in his or her dish.*

Selecting a Boarding Kennel

The boarding kennel remains a popular choice among traveling dog owners with thirty million of them making use of the nation's nine thousand kennels, according to the American Boarding Kennels Association (ABKA), based in Colorado Springs, Colo.

Kennels usually offer individual areas comprised of two enclosures—one for privacy and sleep, the other for exercise and elimination, says Jim Krack, ABKA executive director.

The arrangement at a kennel might appear Spartan but can mimic home life more closely than you'd expect. "Most dogs are very sedentary at home; they're not playing and frolicking," Krack says, noting that dogs who exercise beyond their usual routine when boarding can return home exhausted.

Kennels' advantages include supervision, bathing and grooming, and companionship from other dogs and kennel staff. A burgeoning trend among kennels is to provide dog-play groups. Krack credited the increasing popularity of off-leash dog parks with sparking the movement, which he thinks could soon become commonplace in the industry.

"It's probably the next step in boarding," he says. However, it presents some challenges. "You really have to be good at reading dogs and making sure they can interact without problems."

One kennel making the most of this model is Citizen Canine in Oakland, Calif. The facility is almost always full, despite its forty-two-dollar per night fee. Owner Tina Merrill says a dog-friendly environment and unique mix of services accounted for its success.

At Citizen Canine, dogs have their own indoor rooms with high-tech ventilation and heating and cooling systems. The rooms, complete with elevated beds and blankets, are constructed for privacy with adjacent walls made of double-paned, frosted Fiberglas. They're also made for companionship: most rooms have Dutch doors, so kennel staff passing by can reach in to give a scratch or cuddle.

Dogs make at least three trips a day to an outdoor, fenced yard for play groups, segregated by size and activity level, and supervised by staff members. Citizen Canine allows owners to bring their dog's food and offers services, including agility training, massage and additional, individual playtime.

When you're evaluating kennels, Krack says, minimum requirements should be a clean facility free of potentially dangerous objects; sturdy, well-maintained fencing and gates and dividers between runs; easily cleaned surfaces that don't retain moisture (concrete and tile, for example, rather than wood and plaster); and a knowledgeable, experienced staff. The kennel should also require full immunizations for dogs. You should give your dog a trial stay, even if just for a day, to help him get used to the environment.

"Choose a place where they walk the dogs regularly, have play groups they organize, and allow dogs to have their own possessions," Dr. Dodman says.

One caveat: not every dog is a good candidate for kenneling. If yours is a very young puppy or an anxious, aggressive dog who requires stringent medical care, find another alternative.

See the ABKA checklist below for more factors to consider in selecting a kennel; also, on Page 76 you'll see the code of ethics by which association kennel owners agree to abide.

Kennel Checklist

Take your dog's special needs into account when choosing a kennel. The American Boarding Kennels Association offers this checklist:

■ *The kennel should be clean and neat.*

■ *If staff members won't allow you to see the dog runs personally—strangers' appearances can upset dogs or introduce germs—they should at least let you view them through a window.*

■ *Look for sturdy fencing and gates for security.*

■ *Make sure primary enclosures provide solid dividers between your pet and the other boarders.*

■ *Check that fire-fighting equipment and smoke detectors are present. Ideally, says ABKA Executive Director Jim Krack, the kennel will have an alarm system directly wired to the local fire department.*

■ *Ensure that vaccination is required of all dogs and, if applicable, that parasite control is in effect.*

■ *Make sure your dog will be comfortable. Exercise runs should be protected from the elements. The animal's quarters should have heating and cooling control and adequate ventilation.*

Kennel Code of Ethics

Members of the American Boarding Kennels Association agree to abide by these ethics. To find member kennels, please see **www.abka.com**. *This list appears here with the association's permission.*

Members agree:

■ *to provide conscientious care for the animals entrusted to them, being constantly attentive to their security, safety, and well-being, and to place their welfare above all other business considerations.*

■ *to take every opportunity to learn more about the profession and to improve his or her services.*

■ *to deal honestly and fairly with the public, and to avoid misrepresentation of services.*

■ *to respect the confidence of every customer served.*

■ *to place service to customers and to boarding kennel industry above personal gain.*

■ *to avoid unfair competitive practices, any slander or defamation of competitors, and actions or business practices which would result in dishonor upon or distrust of competitors or of the boarding kennel industry in general.*

■ *to support the association, its policies and programs, and to participate as fully as possible in its activities.*

■ *to be respectful of, and to cooperate with the other professions and trades which operate within the pet industry.*

■ *to obey all applicable federal, state, and local laws governing animal care.*

■ *to operate this business in such a manner as to reflect honor upon the boarding kennel industry within the local community.*

■ *to encourage responsible pet ownership, and to promote, especially through the charitable programs of ABKA, an increased awareness and acceptance of humane and noble animal programs.*

Boarding With a Veterinarian

Many veterinary clinics house dogs, and their rates often are reasonable. If your absence will be short, or if your dog might benefit from medical supervision, this can be a viable alternative. There's also the obvious: "If something should go wrong, there's quick and easy access to a vet," Dr. Berg says.

While many clinics provide exercise and interaction with the staff, some may simply keep dogs in cages or small enclosures. Dr. Dodman, for one, finds this the least appealing boarding option, especially its effect on the dog's psychological well-being.

"The dogs are getting fed, they can relieve themselves, but other than that, they're just sitting there looking at the four walls," he says. "They say that when you confine a person long enough, it's not a question of whether you go mad, it's a question of when. The same goes for dogs."

Go in Peace

Leaving your dog, whether it's the first time or the fiftieth, can be stressful. But take heart from Jim Krack's experience. "In the sixteen years we owned a kennel ... we found boarding for most dogs is not an experience that they dread. They get to know the place, the routine, and they just enjoy it."

Dr. Berg agreed: "Most dogs handle boarding better than most owners think they do. They don't get stressed out. They adjust, they don't panic and think they've been abandoned. Most of those concerns tend to be in the owner's mind." ■

8

Canine Travel

*Help make your dog's trips in the car
or airplane pleasant and safe.*

merica's love affair with the automobile began one hundred years ago, and shows no signs of waning. Our love affair with dogs goes back even further, but sometimes, mixing the two can be hazardous. Some dogs simply are uncomfortable about car rides, even a short trip to run errands, and unrestrained dogs can be tossed about and even killed in case of a sudden stop or accident.

Most owners know better (or should know better) than to let a dog stick his or her head out the car window. The dangers are obvious—the animal's eyes can dry out from the wind or be injured by a projectile; limbs can be damaged when the window is open too far, inviting the dog to attempt to clamber out and follow that inviting scent.

But what if even getting your dog into the car is a nerve-racking experience? What if your dog trembles and cowers at the mere mention of a car trip? Is this a psychological or physiological problem? And, once the dog is in the car, how can your companion ride with you safely?

Psychological or Physiological?

"I imagine there could be a psychological component in the sense that a dog who, through prior experience, learns that car rides make

Danger! This dog's eyes may dry out from the wind or be damaged by debris.

it sick may subsequently become anxious when faced with the prospect of a car ride," says Alice Moon-Fanelli, clinical assistant professor at Tufts University School of Veterinary Medicine.

Others speculate that a balance problem could be to blame. Whatever the cause, motion sickness is common among dogs, especially puppies, said Michael Stone, veterinary internist at Tufts. The good news: "They usually outgrow the problem with time."

Desensitization Techniques

Meanwhile, owners can do their part by making car rides fun—not exclusively devoted to veterinary visits and groomer appointments, where uncomfortable procedures sometimes await. Dogs may associate car rides with the physical discomfort of nausea, noise from passing vehicles, and disequilibrium from winding roads. They seem to do better out on the highway. A possible solution: "In the beginning, go for short rides and pair the ride with a pleasant experience, such as a walk in the park," Dr. Moon-Fanelli says.

If a dog seems overly nervous riding in the car, trainers suggest desensitizing him or her. Begin by sitting together in the car without the engine running ten minutes several days in a row. Stay low key. Pet the dog; give treats. Then for several days, start the engine but don't move the car. Again, give treats. Then drive around the block. Praise and treat. Finally, take longer rides.

When to Get Help

If carsickness persists, seek medical intervention. Dr. Stone commonly prescribes Benadryl, which is sold over the counter. The usual dose for small dogs is one-fourth to one-half of a 25-milligram tablet and one to two tablets for large dogs. Sedation can be a side effect.

If your dog appears healthy, you can give Dramamine, also available without prescription. "I recommend one-fourth to one-half of a 50-mg tablet an hour prior to travel," Dr. Stone says. "The drug may cause mild sedation, but other than that, it is safe and usually effective. You should check with your veterinarian before using either Benadryl or Dramamine."

"Food prior to travel may be either settling or upsetting. It depends on the individual. In most cases, food is tolerated just fine," he says. Never restrict water without a veterinarian's approval.

It should go without saying that a pet locked in a hot car can suffer a fatal heatstroke in less than fifteen minutes. Always allow fresh air into the car, and don't leave pets in the car alone on sunny days even if it doesn't feel warm outside.

Travel Essentials

These items will make life on the road easier for you and your dog:

■ *Paper towels*

■ *Water*

■ *Food and treats*

■ *Flea, tick, and heartworm medications*

■ *Prescription medications*

■ *Toys*

■ *A favorite blanket or dog bed*

- *Folding bowls*

- *Leash*

- *Identification tags*

- *Vaccination records*

- *First aid kit and instructions*

- *Grooming supplies*

- *A current photo of the dog in case he or she becomes lost*

- *Contact information for emergency veterinary care at your destination*

About Restraints

With practice drives behind you and medication, if necessary, you and your dog are ready to take to the road. You'll be wearing your seat belt, and if a youngster is coming along, he or she will be in a car seat. But what about your dog?

First, don't ever let your dog ride in the back of an open truck. In many locations, this is illegal and furthermore, the potential for severe injury is great. Consider the risk of damage to eyes from flying debris, the discomfort from exposure to the elements, the encouragement of aggressive dog behavior, and the real possibility of the animal jumping or falling from the truck.

No reliable statistics are kept on the number of dogs killed or injured in automobile accidents each year. One Colorado veterinarian says that, in a single year, he has seen as many as thirteen dogs killed and close to another sixty injured in auto accidents. Of the forty-thousand-plus persons killed each year in car accidents in the United States, 45 percent might have been saved by seat belts; seat belts also may have reduced serious injuries by 50 percent. Logically, they'd do the same for pets.

The forces generated by even a low-speed collision are tremendous and can be expressed in various ways. If a car is doing 40 mph, unrestrained occupants will continue forward motion at that speed until they hit something. The impact of a 25 mph accident is often compared to falling from a three-story window; in a 30 mph crash, g-forces convert a twenty-pound baby into a six-hundred-pound mass. At the same speed, a sixty-pound dog will impact an object within a foot with a force of a thousand pounds per square inch. Any car restraint must be able to withstand these forces to protect the occupant.

The federal standard for a two-inch seat belt is six thousand pounds of tensile strength. There are no standards for canine restraints, although—to be effective—they must conform to the laws of physics.

Canine restraints serve a number of purposes, including keeping your dog from becoming a missile in the event of an accident as described above. An airborne dog is not only in danger him or herself; the animal also could hit and seriously injure you or a passenger. Restraints also can protect pets from the explosive force of an air bag—although it's safest to strap your dog in on the back seat. Finally, restraints can aid rescue personnel, who sometimes report being held off or attacked by unrestrained and panicked dogs while attempting to perform their duties at the scene of an accident.

It's important to understand that not all canine restraints on the market are intended to serve as seat belts. Several suppliers, in their disclaimers, note that the primary use of their device is to keep a pet under control while riding in the car. That itself is a safety factor; a few years ago. a pickup truck driver who was trying to control his unrestrained Rottweiler lost control of his vehicle and struck and injured best-selling author Stephen King.

There are two basic types of restraints: the canine safety harness and the canine car seat. Typically, these systems utilize car seat belts. In many of today's cars, the front seat belts (and some rear belts) only tighten on impact; during normal travel they expand to allow for passenger comfort. To securely fasten any canine restraint system, you may have to use a rear, solid belt or come up with an alternate strap around the front seat to provide a stable base for the attachment. Unless you are mechanically proficient, have a solid seat belt installed by a professional.

Look for materials that are sturdy and will restrain your pet, yet allow him or her to be freed quickly as needed.

In any event, do not simply attach a vehicle restraint strap to your dog's collar as the primary means of restraint. Although this would work to keep him or her contained during normal travel, in an accident the force of impact could damage the dog's trachea, injure the spine, perhaps even break the neck.

Taking Flight

Consider this statistic: until recent improvements in pet air travel, 1 percent of the half million animals who traveled by air each year died or were lost or injured.

"In the past, it was common practice to ship dogs and cats in the baggage area," says Nicholas Dodman, director of the Behavior Clinic at Tufts University School of Veterinary Medicine. The noisy, dark holds were pressurized but not climate controlled. Pets felt the extremes of heat and cold during flights and as the planes waited on the tarmac or as baggage waited outdoors to make connecting flights.

Temperature extremes alone didn't cause the deaths. In the mid-1990s, U.S. Department of Agriculture veterinarians determined that oversedation accounted for nearly half the animal deaths on airlines, with environmental stress the second most frequent cause. Least common were deaths linked to mishandling by airlines.

Dr. Dodman says the sedative-related deaths had to do with the type of medication prescribed. "Acepromazine was introduced to veterinary medicine in 1951," he says. "... But one of the things acepromazine does is lower body temperature" and just a few degrees can make a difference when a dog is exposed to low temperatures.

Researchers aren't sure how dogs react physiologically to sedatives at an altitude of eight thousand feet and the air pressure in passenger cabins and baggage holds. As an alternative, he prescribes an anxiety-reduction medication, buspirone, which also reduces motion sickness. Owners should consult veterinarians about what's best for a particular dog.

The American Animal Hospital Association recommends considering whether the pet is temperamentally suited to air travel without medication; the International

Air Transport Association, a trade organization for commercial airlines outside the United States, advises against sedating pets even if they'll fly in the passenger cabin. Some airlines won't accept sedated pets.

It's also important to keep in mind that beyond the question of sedation, some airlines accept only small pets who can be carried in the passenger cabin and others refuse pets altogether.

No matter how they fly, canine air travelers must be at least eight weeks old and fully weaned. The USDA requires that they be offered food and water within four hours of check-in. Airlines also require health and rabies certificates showing the dog was examined by a veterinarian no more than ten days before travel.

Canine Carriers

Pet carriers often provide the most comfort for dogs traveling in cars, according to the American Animal Hospital Association. The carrier should allow the dog to stand up or lie down, should have nothing sticking into the interior, be well ventilated and have a rim around the outside that keeps other objects from blocking the airflow.

While on the Road

Your dog typically can maintain his or her regular schedule during car travel, says Tufts' Dr. Stone.

"For a healthy dog, traveling in a car poses little difference to their daily routine," he says. "If a dog normally walks twice a day and eliminates twice a day, a car ride for twelve hours shouldn't be a big deal. Walking as frequently as every four to six hours is recommended." Remember that most pets defecate within thirty minutes of eating, and plan the feeding accordingly, Dr. Stone says.

It's usually not necessary to bring water from home, Dr. Stone says. However, some owners notice that their dogs experience digestive upset from water in a new location, just as people do, so they take water.

Water cannot offset the evils of leaving a dog in a closed car. "Owners shouldn't leave animals in the car with windows closed in any weather condition," he says, because even in cool weather, sunshine raises a car's interior temperature dangerously high within minutes.

Unlike people, dogs do not perspire throughout their bodies but only through their paws, which is not enough to effectively cool them in high humidity, especially in a closed car. The most omportant way dogs control their body temperature is through panting, and they may not be able to pant enough in a closed car to stay cool.

Weigh the potential risks and problems and your ability to resolve them before taking your dog on a car trip, long or short. Sometimes, says Kim Christoffersen of **www.traveldog.com**, a Web sit with information about traveling with dogs, "you have to leave them home." ■

9

Putting Out the Fire

Preventing—and dealing with—
your dog's painful and itchy "hot spots."

Hot spots are one of the leading causes of visits to the veterinarian. Known by the technical term pyotraumatic dermatitis, they indicate a range of conditions for inflamed skin or infected sores. The infection can be superficial or quite deep. A hot spot can mean a small area that your dog scratches repeatedly that heals after application of a topical ointment, or it can be one that rapidly expands to the size of your palm. Unfortunately, the onset of each type looks the same.

"There are two common forms of hot spots," says Michael Stone, assistant clinical professor and veterinary internist at Tufts University School of Veterinary Medicine. "One is related to self-itching and clears up best with clipping, cleaning, prednisone, and possibly with topical products, Elizabethan collars, and sedatives. The other form, which looks exactly the same to an untrained eye, is actually a deep bacterial infection of the skin. In these cases, clipping and cleaning along with antibiotic therapy are necessary."

Common signs of hot spots are hair loss and itching, and scratching that leads to self-induced skin lesions. The lesions are often red, oozing, painful, and itchy. Sometimes they become crusty or scaly. "The owner may notice the dog biting or scratching frequently at a particular area or may notice a foul odor," Dr. Stone says.

Sometimes hair mats over the lesion so that it's not immediately noticed. If the spot is painful, even a normally complacent dog may growl when touched. Some hot spots are painful enough to require that the dog wear a muzzle during the veterinary examination, so be careful if you're examining your dog at home.

Early Treatment

Treating the lesions early will help minimize exudates, or extruded matter, says Gene Nesbitt, consulting dermatologist at Tufts Dermatology and Allergy Service. "The exudate on the surface is secondary to the trauma. It is both a break in the surface barrier allowing leakage of fluids onto the surface and the colonization of the bacteria on the surface."

Hot spots develop as a result of flea infestation, environmental or food allergies, irritants, foreign bodies, otitis (inflammation of the ear), anal sac infections, psychoses, or underlying musculoskeletal pain, Dr. Nesbitt says. Your veterinarian will look for parasites, such as fleas, mites or even insect stings. He'll ask about allergies and look for small skin scrapes or similar small injuries that could cause itching. Psychological causes are common; bored or stressed dogs often scratch themselves.

Cutaneous parasites, such as mange, can also lead to hot spots, Dr. Stone says. "This is a small percentage of total cases but should be considered in cases that don't respond to appropriate therapy or that recur frequently."

Hot spots differ from other types of dermatitis. The condition is not considered a primary skin infection, says Dr. Nesbitt. "Hot spots may look similar to other types of dermatitis if acute onset, well-demarcated focal areas are involved, and self-trauma is always a predisposing cause."

Because the lesions are pruritic (itchy) and/or painful, steroids are usually indicated, he says. "Some lesions may need a steroid with a strong anti-inflammatory effect. If there is deeper skin involvement with secondary bacterial infection, antibiotics will also be prescribed."

Dogs with a dense hair coat tend to be predisposed. Golden Retrievers, Labs, Collies, German Shepherds and St. Bernards are often most severely affected.

The goal of treatment is to relieve the pain and itching to prevent scratching, control the infection and let the spot heal. Afterward, the hair should grow back normally, although in rare cases the skin can scar.

Clipping the lesion is usually the first step, followed by a gentle but thorough cleaning with an antibacterial agent, such as iodine or

Dogs with a dense haircoat like this St. Bernard (above) tend to be predisposed to hot spots, along with Golden Retrievers, Labs, Collies, and German Shepherds.

In addition to being unsightly and very painful, hot spots may be an indication that the dog's immune system is failing to protect the dog adequately from bacteria.

chlorhexidine, Dr. Nesbitt says.

The itch-scratch cycle must be broken, so corticosteroids are often used for short-term relief. The application of a drying agent like Burow's solution or other anti-inflammatory/antibacterial agents is generally indicated. Topical steroids are generally indicated if they are not being administered systemically."

Dogs are very uncomfortable when the hot spot area is touched, and sedation is frequently necessary to clip and clean, Dr. Stone says, adding that pain relievers usually aren't necessary and discomfort resolves after twelve to twenty-four hours.

Apply Compresses

After cleansing, cool compresses should be used two to four times a day. The veterinarian may recommend topical drying sprays and specific shampoos. The type of shampoo depends upon the predisposing and concurrent problems. If the hair isn't clipped, an antibacterial shampoo will help clean the surface. Once the lesion is cleaned and the self-trauma controlled, shampoos will have minimal effect on the healing lesion.

It's common for a dog to have hot spots only once in a lifetime, but some dogs get them repeatedly. "There's no truly chronic pyotraumatic dermatitis," says Dr. Stone. "A chronic skin lesion should be evaluated for infection or other underlying condition."

Restrictions during treatment are minor. "Immediately after discharge, the dog should be confined until resolution is fairly obvious—in one to two days," he says. "After improvement is noted, no restrictions are usually necessary."

Unfortunately, there's no specific way to prevent hot spots. "Maintain preventative flea control and good grooming," Dr. Stone says. "Treat any chronic underlying problem, such as allergies, otitis or psychoses." And, he adds, closely examine your dog for early lesions. ■

10

Hot & Cold
Weather Care

*Every season brings its own set of
concerns and cautions for dog owners.*

Caring for our dogs is a year-round job, but our canine pals
have different need and care requirements depending on
the season. Summer brings warmth and longer days, and
with that comes the risk of heatstroke, dehydration, ticks,
and fleas. Winter, with shorter daylight hours and colder temperatures, requires extra caution when walking our pets at night, and
extra care for their snow- and ice-exposed feet. Springtime is shedding time, and in fall the days grow short and visibility again becomes a concern.

Sun Sense

Just as for humans, early summer is a great time for dogs. Getting
out to play, especially after being cooped up for months, is a joy.
But balancing summer recreation with heat safety is serious business for dogs. As any critical care veterinarian will tell you, heatstroke is one of the summer's most frequent—and most lethal—
canine afflictions.

In summer's extreme heat, it's best to restrict your dog's outdoor
activities to the cooler hours of morning and evening. One important reason for this is to protect footpads from being burned on hot
black asphalt, which can absorb enough heat during the day to injure the extra-thick flesh on your dog's paws. A rule of thumb about

hot sidewalks and driveways: don't ask your dog to walk on pavement that you would not cross in your bare feet.

Anyone who cares for a snub-nosed, or brachycephalic breed of dog, such as a Pekingese, pug, or English bulldog, should seriously consider the purchase of an indoor cooling system for the summer months if the home or apartment doesn't already have one. Due to a malformation of the soft palate, such dogs are less able to cool themselves by panting. They can actually exhaust themselves and worsen the situation with their panting, a situation some people call call *ineffectual panter syndrome.*

Sunburn is also a concern for your dog. With lighter skinned dogs, it is wiser to keep a longer coat in the summer for protection against the sun. Some dog owners even opt to have lightly pigmented areas tattooed or tinted with ink to make them less vulnerable to the sun's rays. For example, the pink rims of a white pit bull terrier's eyes are particularly susceptible to sunburn and could benefit from artificial pigmentation—a procedure performed only by a reliable veterinarian.

Dogs, too, can suffer serious sunburns. Some owners find that dressing a dog in a loose, white T-shirt or providing a source of shade such as a beach umbrella for extended outdoor periods works well. If your dog does suffer a burn, apply cool towels to the irritated skin and use an aloe vera preparation. Keep in mind that many topical ointments induce licking, which will further aggravate damaged skin.

The Danger of Heatstroke

The worst case scenario for any dog is to suffer heatstroke. Certain dogs by virtue of heredity or life history may be particularly vulnerable. Any pet with a history of heatstroke will be more susceptible, and you should make appropriate preventive measures. When a dog suffers heatstroke, his or her internal temperature soars, possibly up to 110 degrees, potenially causing irreversible brain damage and/or death. Symptoms might include: elevated body temperature, vigorous panting, unsteady gait, physical depression or agitation, thick saliva or froth at the nose or mouth, rigid posture, muddy mucous membranes, (delayed capillary refill time) vomiting, bloody diarrhea, collapsing, and signs of shock.

Treating heatstroke involves cooling the dog from the inside out.

■ First, the dog should be removed from the source of heat to cooler surroundings, such as a room indoors, with a fan directed on

This Chow gets a lion cut each summer to help her stay cool.

his or her body, or the breezy shade of a tree.

■ Then the dog's entire body should be dampened with cool (never cold) water, keeping in mind that when only the surface areas of the body are cooled, the superficial blood vessels restrict, forming an insulating layer that actually traps heat deeper inside. Ice packs should be restricted to the head, neck and chest.

■ While tempting the dog to drink cool water or to lick ice cubes, don't force him or her to consume water orally. In a state of shock, choking could result. Instead, concentrate on keeping the dog's immediate surroundings cool, monitor vital signs and contact a veterinarian as soon as possible. Heatstroke always requires immediate professional supervision.

More Summer Hazards

Lawn Chemical Safeguards

For dogs and people who have been hibernating all winter, spring offers an irresistible invitation to frolic outdoors. But spring also signals the beginning of chemical warfare against lawn-wrecking bugs and weeds. When used as directed, lawn chemicals rarely cause acute poisoning, but scientists know little about the long-term effects of exposure to these chemicals. Help safeguard your dog's long-term health by following these guidelines to minimize his or her exposure to lawn chemicals:

■ Store lawn-care chemicals away from your dog and carefully follow the manufacturer's directions when mixing and applying these chemicals. Remove any puddles or piles of chemicals on the lawn, driveway, or sidewalk.

■ Keep your dog off the lawn until the chemicals have thoroughly soaked in—that means waiting twenty-four hours for liquids, and longer for granules.

■ Make a list of the chemicals you or your lawn-care company apply to your lawn. Your veterinarian will want to know what chemicals your dog may have been exposed to if the animal becomes ill. And check with town or city officials to see what chemicals are applied to the public areas where you walk your dog.

■ Keep your dog on a leash or confined to your yard to prevent him or her from getting into your neighbor's chemical arsenal.

Water Hazards

During the sweltering dog days of summer, dogs sometimes plunge into swimming pools or ponds to beat the heat. Alas, drowning due to exhaustion can occur if a dog can't get out of a pool or a steeply banked natural body of water.

To avoid tragedy:

■ Don't let your dog run at large.

■ If you own a pool, install a secure fence around it and never let your dog wander inside the pool area unsupervised. Also, show your dog where the shallow-end steps are and how to use them.

In case of accident:

■ If the dog is unconscious, place the animal on an incline with the head tilted downward, pull the tongue forward, and gently push on the animal's chest to help clear the airway of water.

■ Check for heartbeat and breathing. If either has stopped, initiate resuscitation while someone else drives the dog to the nearest veterinarian.

Lifesaving Reminders

It never ceases to appall the conscientious caregiver to see a dog locked inside of a car in the summer heat. This is a veritable death sentence, since the temperature inside of a baking car can soar to 120 degrees, even with the windows partially open. The sun's shifting makes parking in the shade unreliable. If it's uncomfortably hot for the driver, it's dangerous for a dog.
Never hesitate to contact your local animal control officer through the police department if you suspect that immediate intervention is warranted. If a pet gets overheated:

■ *Get the animal into some shade and apply cool (not cold) water all over the body.*

■ *Apply ice packs or cold towels only to head, neck and chest.*

■ *Let the dog drink small amounts of cool water, or lick ice cubes or ice cream.*

■ *Get your pet to a veterinarian right away—it could save his or her life.*

■ *Remember, on hot days, your pet is safer at home!*

Spring: Surviving Shedding Season

We all relish the warmer, longer days of spring. But increased daylight is a major trigger for the four- to five-week spring shedding season. "During the spring, hair follicles [the cavities out of which hair grows] that were resting all winter go through a growth spurt, and new hairs push out the old ones," says Dr. Richard Anderson, a Boston area retired dermatologist who was with Angell Animal Medical Center.

Because shedding is a normal physiological process for most dogs (except for poodles, some wire-haired terriers, and a handful of other breeds that have continuously growing, humanlike hair), there's not much you can do about it other than help the process along. Start with a bath. Keep in mind that none of the "antishedding" potions available from pet-supply catalogs and stores have been clinically proven to reduce shedding. "It's bathing and grooming, rather than any active ingredient in a lotion or shampoo, that alleviates shedding," says Dr. Anderson.

If you're brave enough to tackle the bathing process at home, keep your dog's safety in mind. Place a towel or rubber mat in the bottom of the tub so your dog doesn't slip, and give your dog—and yourself—periodic time outs to rest.

After drying your dog, use a combination of tools (depending on what kind of coat your dog has) to remove more dead hair. The most popular utensil for brushing out long- and thick-coated dogs is the wire-pin slicker brush, and steel-tined grooming rakes are good for removing hair from dogs with densely packed undercoats. But do take care, because overzealous use of these tools can hurt your dog's skin.

Although fur will inevitably fly during shedding season, there are several ways to repel or remove dog hair from clothing and furniture. Some people find an anti-static spray helps repelling hair from car seats and clothing. You can also buy hair-pickup rollers and gloves, but a regular old lint brush or adhesive packing tape works just as well. With their large surface area, the adhesive backs of overnight-package airbill pouches also work wonders.

Cold-Weather Cautions

Chemicals and Ice

Even in balmy climes, the mercury falls in fall and winter.. Here's how to dodge some outdoor wintertime dog hazards:

■ **Ice Balls:** These painful paw-pad problems occur when cold snow crystallizes upon contact with warm, furry dog feet.Trim the hair between your dog's foot pads. If your dog develops "frozen feet," melt the ice balls with a warm, moist face cloth.

■ **Road Salt:** Many cities and towns treat icy streets and sidewalks with potentially irritating salts. Wash your dog's paws after walking in areas treated with ice-melting compounds. Discourage your dog from chewing or licking his or her feet after a walk through road salt and keep the animal away from chemical deicers stored in your home.

Walking in the Dark

Along with crisp autumn air come earlier sunsets and later sunrises. This means your morning and evening dog walks may soon be shrouded in darkness. You can't rely on your pet's tapetum lucidum (a layer in the canine eyeball that makes a dog's eyes shine with reflected light) to brighten your path. But there are several reliable ways to keep you and your pet safe during your darkened forays:

■ Leash your dog and keep the animal close to your side at all times.

■ Using ID tags, tattoos, or microchips, make sure your dog can be easily identified for prompt return if, by chance, the two of you are separated.

■ Make sure you and your dog are highly visible. Use passive-illumination devices such as reflective collars and vests for your dog and reflective footwear and clothing for yourself. Consider battery-powered active illumination for greater protection. Devices range from hand-held or strapped-on lanterns to retractable leashes with flashlights built into the handle and flashing safety collars. Not only will these devices alert passing motorists, they will also announce your presence to other animals and possibly prevent unwanted encounters with wandering wildlife.

■ Above all, prevent your dog from running at large in *all* seasons. ■

11

Breathing Easy

*That heavy panting could indicate overexertion
and possibly heatstroke, or a breed-related problem.
Learn how to spot the symptoms of trouble.*

Your dog enjoyed a rousing session of Frisbee on a hot afternoon. Now he's sitting in the shade, panting heavily. Or, maybe after a period of inactivity, he suddenly seems weak and begins to pant. Which case is cause for concern? Actually, either scenario could indicate a medical emergency or illness.

"Lots of panting can be an early sign of potential heatstroke," says Elizabeth Rozanski, a specialist in emergency and critical care medicine and assistant professor at Tufts University School of Veterinary Medicine who has a special interest in respiratory disease. "Therefore, on a hot day, excessive panting is not to be taken lightly. Any breathing problems or perceived breathing problems require treatment.

Healthy dogs pant for one simple reason: to cool down. Their only sweat glands are on their footpads. "Dogs with normal panting usually have just participated in an activity that could make them hot and are relatively easily distracted from panting—like with a biscuit," Dr. Rozanski says.

Heatstroke Symptoms

If, however, a dog overexerts himself or herself in warm weather or the animal is inappropriately left in a parked car long enough to raise the body temperature above 104 degrees Fahrenheit, your pet will be a potential candidate for heatstroke. An affected dog will pant heavily and drool. The gums will become pale, then deep red. Your pet will become disoriented, suffering vomiting and diarrhea and lapse into a coma with possible damage to the brain and other organs.

This life-threatening condition requires that an owner immerse the dog in cool—not cold—water to lower the animal's temperature while veterinary help is sought. In his book, *Caring for Your Dog: The Complete Canine Home Reference* (DK Publishing), veterinarian Bruce Fogle suggests placing a bag of frozen peas, wrapped in cloth, on the dog's head to reduce heat around the brain.

Veterinarians often treat heatstroke, or hyperthermia, by giving oxygen and intravenous fluids if the patient is dehydrated.

About Brachycephalic Breeds

Brachycephalic dogs—those with flat noses such as Bulldogs, Pekingese, Shar-Peis, Shih Tzus, Cavalier King Charles Spaniels, and Pugs—are especially vulnerable to heatstroke, as are overweight dogs.

"They are unable to cool effectively, and this is magnified if they are overweight, Dr. Rozanski says.

Some brachycephalic dogs suffer from an overly long soft palate—the fleshy part at the back of the mouth that forms part of its roof—or a partial blockage of airflow from the nares, or nostrils, to the throat. They also may have small trachea or everted laryngeal sacs that block the airway. In some brachycephalic dogs, the larynx has collapsed.

These animals have to work harder than other dogs to breathe. Signs of brachycephalic airway syndrome include noisy breathing with an open mouth, snoring and panting. It's easy to see the dogs' stomachs move up and down when they breathe. The breathing muscles are overdeveloped because of the extra effort it takes to breathe. Many of the dogs are exercise-intolerant. Some vomit and have difficulty eating.

"This condition results from the facial conformation," said John Berg, veterinary surgeon and chair of TUVSM's Department of Clinical Sciences. "Not all brachycephalic dogs have breathing problems."

Breeds like these with flat noses are especially vulnerable to heatstroke.

Your dog should be evaluated to determine if the problem is severe enough to require surgery (usually a minor procedure to shorten the dog's soft palate). "If they try to exercise and run out of energy or breath, or if they have a difficult time going to sleep because of breathing, or they tend to get overheated and restless in warm weather, they usually have a problem," Dr. Berg says.

The difficulties become noticeable when the dog is reluctant to walk or slows down, makes even more noise than usual, or the mucus membranes turn bluish. If that happens, the dog should be taken to a cool place and calmed down. Typically, the dog will be fine; the condition rarely calls for emergency veterinary visits.

Other Problems Signaled by Panting

Panting, along with lethargy or weakness, can also be a sign of pneumonia, heart disease, Cushing's disease, pleural effusion (fluid in the chest cavity), anemia, nasal blockages, collapsing trachea, and various types of cancer within the chest cavity. Some drugs, such as corticosteroids, can affect the respiratory centers in the brain and cause panting, Dr. Rozanski says. And, some dogs will pant simply because they are excited or anxious.

Heavy panting is also a sign of eclampsia in dogs who have given birth. Those who are smaller or undernourished or who have had large litters can develop the condition, caused by milk production depleting calcium in their bodies. Dogs with eclampsia need immediate veterinary care to prevent death.

Though it's difficult to distinguish different kinds of panting, the healthy from the labored, owners may avoid some emergencies associated with the later.

"Prevent heatstroke and overexertion," Dr. Rozanski says. "Know your dog's normal respiratory rate and gum color. Check the tongue; a pink tongue indicates plenty of oxygen in the blood. And I would reiterate any breathing problems or perceived breathing problems require a visit to your veterinarian." ■

12

Petting With a Purpose

Just like humans, dogs derive physical and emotional benefits from massage. Learn how and why.

Whether your dog qualifies as a field trial champion or a couch potato, he or she can derive benefits from massage. In fact, all our canine friends—including those with demanding jobs, those with a more leisurely lifestyle, and those with chronic problems that hinder activity—can benefit from massage.

"The skin is the biggest sensory organ in the body," said C. Sue Furman, associate professor in the department of anatomy and neurobiology at the School of Veterinary Medicine at Colorado State University in Fort Collins and the author of *Canine Massage: Balance Your Dog* (Wolfchase Publishing). "The receptors in the skin react biochemically to being touched. If positive touch is applied on a dog's skin, the receptors signal the brain to release endorphins—feel-good hormones. If the touch is negative, the dog can react by tensing its muscles, recoiling out of fear or even being defensively aggressive."

Canine massage has the potential to benefit a dog's skeletal, muscular, nervous, circulatory, lymphatic, endocrine, respiratory, digestive and urinary systems, according to the American Veterinary Medical Association. Tufts University School of Veterinary Medicine also recognizes the benefit of therapeutic touch and has a physical therapist on staff.

"This is an indicator of the value of purposeful touch, particularly during recovery from orthopedic and neurologic conditions," says Dr. John Berg, chair of TUVSM's Department of Clinical Sciences.

Some massage therapists incorporate acupressure or other therapies into their dog massage routines.

What Is Canine Massage?

Massage is a hands-on manipulation of the muscles and other soft tissues with the intent of benefiting the animal. Massage is touch with a purpose, and it yields many physical and emotional benefits.

Physically, massage stimulates circulation, enhances range of motion, relieves muscle spasms and encourages a healthier coat, and improves flexibility. The positive effects on mental attitude and emotions are just as important. For example, massage promotes relaxation, reduces stress, fosters a sense of well-being, and strengthens the bond between human and animal.

Massage, which to the casual observer appears to range from gentle stroking to more vigorous kneading and percussion of tissues, affects the dog physically and emotionally by markedly influencing the nerve, muscle, circulatory, and lymph systems. None of the body's systems works in isolation. It is estimated that the human body has sixty thousand miles of capillaries. Dogs have a proportionately similar amount, taking into consideration the size difference between a Chihuahua and Great Dane. Each muscle fiber or cell is surrounded by three or four of these tiny blood vessels that bring oxygen and nutrients to the cells and carry away waste products.

The nervous system communicates with each muscle cell through neurons (or nerve cells) that carry messages to the brain indicating whether the muscle is relaxed, contracted, or injured. Similarly, messages return to the muscles and stimulate them to respond by contracting or relaxing.

Massage enhances circulation by stimulating the movement of blood through the capillaries. Stimulation by massage also enhances muscle tone. Tiny areas of muscle in spasm are encouraged to relax and the overall health of muscle and nerve are improved.

Also, massage relaxes your dog just as a massage or even a good shoulder and back rub relaxes your tight muscles when you are stressed. Massage also affects the capillaries that nourish the skin with oxygen and nutrients and cleanse it of wastes and toxins. This can improve the health of the skin.

> 66 MASSAGE IS TOUCH WITH A PURPOSE AND IT YIELDS MANY PHYSICAL AND EMOTIONAL BENEFITS. 99

The Mind/Muscle Connection

In some ways, your dog's body works just like yours. Muscles can become tight, sore, stiff, or flaccid due to overuse or disuse. Emotional stress can also affect your dog's muscles and general well-being. How does your dog react to potentially stressful situations like a trip to the vet, separation from you, or an encounter with an unfamiliar dog? Like humans, part of a dog's response to stress may manifest as tense, tight muscles. Massage can go a long way to reverse the adverse results of stress-producing events by relieving this tension. It can also greatly enhance your bond with your dog.

Keep in mind that the systems of the body work together as an integrated unit. Events—good or bad—that impact one system lead to a cascade of effects that eventually impact all systems.

A "Whole Body" Dynamic

Consider, for example, what happens if your dog cuts a paw. Certainly, there will be some loss of blood and infection-fighting white

Without regular hands-on massage sessions, this older, slightly arthritic dog develops tight, knotted muscles, and becomes cranky with pain.

blood cells will rush to the area. The involvement of the circulatory system is obvious. Then the area surrounding the cut will swell with cellular fluids released due to the damage. Next, the lymphatic system will swing into action to decrease the swelling by removing the excess fluid and carrying off other cellular debris resulting from the injury.

Because the dog's paw is sore, he or she may compensate for the pain by limping or shifting weight from one part of the body to another. This can stress healthy joints and muscles, causing them to become misaligned and strained and to suffer abnormal wear and tear. The pain also may lower the dog's spirits and dampen his or her appetite.

Just as a minor cut can upset the body's balance and affect some aspect of virtually every system, massage can bring about positive changes to many systems of the body. An open wound should never be directly massaged. In fact, any wound care you do at home should be done only after seeking the advice of a veterinarian.

How to Do It

When you're ready to try massaging your dog, aim for a time when the two of you can be uninterrupted. Find a quiet, cozy area.

"Never force massage on a dog," Dr. Furman says. "Always greet your dog in a friendly way. The first touch can establish a feeling of trust that leads to relaxation and a rewarding experience to both you and your dog. Read your dog's body cues, and stop if your dog is showing signs that he wants to leave by tensing his muscles or wiggling."

Canine massage involves different types of strokes. Some of the more common ones are explained below.

Passive Touch

This is an introductory stroke to your dog to initiate a massage in a welcoming way. With the animal resting on the ground, gently and confidently place both hands on the back. Hold it for several seconds before slowly moving both hands to a new position until your dog gets used to this type of touch.

Effleurage

This term comes from the French word *effleure*, which means to glide over the surface. Use an open hand to slide over your dog's coat in a long, purposeful motion.

Digital Stroking

This is done with a very gentle, light touch using your fingertips. You stroke the length of your dog from neck to tail. The fingertips should travel over the coat at a rate of one to two inches per second.

Compression

Dogs with tense, sore muscles benefit from this rhythmic pumping motion with your open palms. Use light pressure on the first stroke and gradually increase the pressure slightly with each subsequent stroke.

Petrissage

The term comes from the French *petrir*, which means to knead or mash. This type of rhythmic stroke rolls, squeezes, wrings, and lifts soft tissue to flush out metabolic waste and toxins while attracting nutrient-carrying oxygenated blood into this area.

Percussion

This stroke uses patting motions. Use your hands or parts of your hand to deliver rapid, springy blows to your dog's body to rhythmically compress the affected tissue area. Percussion can be light or heavy and primarily benefits the nervous and circulatory systems.

Stretching

The elongating of muscle tissues increases a dog's flexibility and range of motion and also decreases tension in muscles and increases circulation. Be careful when stretching your dog's limbs. Don't do it too rapidly or too far, or you could tear muscles and tendons.

Studies Show Touch's Positive Effects

The Touch Research Institutes at the University of Miami School of Medicine has conducted more than ninety studies on the effects of massage therapy on people from newborns to the elderly. Researchers have included representatives from Harvard, Duke, Maryland, and other universities.

Among the health benefits, the researchers have found that massage:

■ *warms body tissues*

■ *increases circulation and blood flow*

■ *improves range of motion*

■ *enhances comfort level*

■ *reduces swelling*

■ *soothes achy, tired muscles*

■ *decreases anxiety and uneasiness*

The studies are available in professional journals, at university libraries, and at **www.miami.edu/ touch-research**.

A Complement, Not a Substitute

Massage is not a substitute for conventional veterinary care but can often be very effectively used in conjunction with conventional care to provide maximum benefit to your dog. There are times when massage is contraindicated. As noted, one should never massage an open wound. Similarly, massage is contraindicated over surgical sites, insect bites, and skin infections. Massage is also inappropriate for an animal who has a temperature or swollen lymph glands, or cancer, is in a state of shock, or has a broken bone or ruptured disk. These conditions require conventional veterinary care. However, your veterinarian might recommend massage as part of the treatment of neurological or muscular-skeletal problems.

When massaging your dog, think of yourself as a music conductor, Dr. Furman says. Consider choreographing a series of individual strokes to reap the most benefits.

"The strokes should never be random but, rather, specifically orchestrated with a basic plan in mind," she says. "However, always listen to what your dog and his muscles tell you as you proceed, and be ready to adjust your plan to meet your dog's needs. Your reward will be a happy, trusting, healthy dog who bonds with you." ■

13

Try This at Home?

For some injuries, a little tender loving care at home will suffice. Other times, not taking your dog to the veterinarian immediately can be life threatening.

When your dog is hurt, you have no time to lose. Your pet needs your attention. Now. Considering the many scrapes and tussles a typical dog will endure in a long, eventful lifetime, it's good to know that you safely can handle some of his or her health problems by at home. But which ones? And how? And which situations definitely require a veterinarian's immediate attention?

While pet owners learn various home remedies from friends and others over time, you may be surprised to learn that veterinarians consider some to be potentially dangerous to dogs. Use soap or hydrogen peroxide on a wound? No, veterinarians say. The chemicals can be harmful. Remove a tick is by touching it with a lighted match, so that it will back out of your dog's body? Wrong. It doesn't work. And you could burn your dog. Use a tourniquet to stop bleeding? Only as a last resort and only if you loosen it frequently.

When a dog experiences a soft tissue injury—a broad term covering a range of internal and external injuries from a minor scratch to a bruised lung—it can be difficult to determine if a veterinary visit is in order. While many dogs occasionally sustain minor scratches, abrasions, or bruises, more serious soft tissue injuries usually involve trauma, such as being struck by a car, being involved in a dog fight or falling from high places, which could include a small dog's jump from an owner's arms to the floor.

Injury to a dog's skin—such as a laceration (a ragged tear), abrasion (the skin is rubbed or scraped away), or cut—is probably the most obvious type of soft tissue injury because it's the most visible. Sometimes, however, a long or dark coat will make a wound difficult to see. Skin injuries may look bad, but in a healthy dog, healing is rarely a problem. The biggest concern is prevention of infection.

Owners can wash, disinfect, and bandage minor cuts, scrapes, and bruises, but a veterinarian can best determine the extent of injury presented by more major wounds. In cases of trauma, sudden lameness, or breathing difficulty, always take your dog to the veterinarian. Be aware that sometimes, dogs suffer traumas that aren't apparent to their owners.

Still, it's possible to deal with some situations at home. Some common dog care issues and solutions follow.

Superficial Wounds

Maybe you just noticed dried blood on your dog, and, beneath it, a superficial wound. What should you do? "Clean the wound. Clean the wound. Clean the wound," says D.J. Krahwinkel, professor of small animal surgery at the University of Tennessee College of Veterinary Medicine.

Use a lot of lukewarm running water in the bathtub and an antibiotic ointment. Don't use soap, hydrogen peroxide, or iodine. "The chemicals may make it worse," Dr. Krahwinkel says.

Wrap the wound with gauze, though not too tightly. Remove the dressing every day and clean the wound with lukewarm water, apply antibiotic ointment, and wrap with new gauze. When in doubt, see a veterinarian.

Wounds that are healing well will gradually fill with pink tissue and shrink in size. "See your veterinarian if the wound starts to drain, particularly if the drainage is thick or the wound doesn't seem to be healing within a week," advises John Berg, veterinary surgeon and chair of the Department of Clinical Sciences at Tufts University School of Veterinary Medicine.

Bite Wounds

Bite wounds often are deeper than they appear on the surface. Also, they're often contaminated with bacteria and debris.

"With bite wounds, you often only see a puncture, but the underlying soft tissue trauma is much greater," says Dr. Berg. "Also, a mouth has a lot of bacteria, so bite wounds are particularly prone to being infected, and extensive bite wounds can even cause life-threatening infections." Signs of infection include redness in the injured area, swelling, and behavioral changes such as lethargy or refusal to eat.

Bite wounds that are associated with bleeding should be evaluated by a veterinarian, says Elizabeth Rozanski, a specialist in emergency and critical care medicine and assistant professor at Tufts.. "Very superficial wounds may be cleaned with warm water on a paper towel," she says.

If the bite was caused by a domesticated animal, be sure to find out the status of the biter's rabies vaccination so you can advise your veterinarian. If you take your dog to an emergency clinic, take along his or her rabies certificate.

Skunk Spray

What should you do if your inquisitive dog ends up sprayed by a skunk? You can try a home remedy although "none work that well," says Tufts' Dr. Rozanski.

Rinse the dog's eyes with plain water or an eyewash solution, the same over-the-counter product that humans use. Mix one-fourth cup baking soda, one teaspoon of liquid soap and one quart of hydrogen peroxide (3 percent solution). Apply to the haircoat; rinse thoroughly.

The better known home remedy involves tomato juice— lots of it. Wash and dry the pet before pouring on several cans of tomato juice. Let the juice soak into the fur for at least ten minutes. Rinse. Wash with dog shampoo again. Repeat the tomato juice, as needed.

Bleeding

Run-of-the-mill cuts and scrapes can be cared for entirely at home. To stop the bleeding, firmly press a clean washcloth, towel or thick gauze pad against the bleeding area. Don't let up. Apply pressure continuously until the bleeding stops, meaning at least ten minutes. Then apply an over-the-counter triple antibiotic ointment such as Neosporin to prevent infection.

Get to veterinarian immediately if the dog suffers from severe blood loss or deep wounds that go beyond the upper skin layers to reach muscle or tendons. To keep pressure on the bleeding area during the imperative trip to the veterinarian, wrap gauze or tape, such as duct tape, around the washcloth or other dressing. "An old washcloth with tape works well for the drive to the hospital," Dr. Rozanski says.

If severe bleeding occurs when you and your dog are hiking, camping, hunting, or are otherwise in a remote location far from a veterinarian, you should muzzle the dog, then firmly press a thick gauze pad over the wound until the bleeding stops and you can get to a veterinarian. If blood soaks through the gauze pad, don't remove it. Add a second or third pad on top. The idea is to layer more gauze around the wound so that you don't strip away any clot that is trying to form. A clean towel or washcloth can be used to stop bleeding, but a thick gauze pad is the best option, said James Ross, Tufts distinguished professor and veterinary cardiologist.

If a leg is bleeding particularly severely, you can slow the flow by pressing firmly on a pressure point located in the upper inside of that leg. If it is impossible to get to a veterinarian until many hours or even days later, then proceed with steps described earlier. If the bleeding stops, clean the wound with lukewarm water. Apply an antibiotic ointment to prevent infection. Wrap the wound with gauze. Daily, remove the bandage to clean the wound and reapply antibiotic ointment.

Only in highly unusual, life-threatening situations should a tourniquet be considered to stop bleeding. It's better to apply direct pressure to the wound by using a gauze pad. Tourniquets are dangerous, Dr. Ross stresses, because they too often cause permanent disability or result in amputation of a limb because the dog's blood supply was cut off for too long. If a tourniquet must be used, apply it between the heart and the wound and loosen it for twenty seconds every fifteen to twenty minutes.

Muzzling is a precautionary step so that your frightened dog won't bite you. Small dogs can be wrapped in a towel or blanket, but don't wrap so tightly that the animal can't breathe. If you don't have a muzzle for your larger dog, use a long length of gauze (a non-stretchy type) or ribbon. The object is to wrap the gauze around the dog's muzzle, pull the ends back, and tie the ends behind his or her ears.

Washington State University's College of Veterinary Medicine recommends doing it this way: Because gauze isn't very strong, double it to increase its strength. Take the long length of gauze and tie a loose square knot at the center, forming a loose loop that is about three times the diameter of the dog's muzzle. Place the loose loop around the dog's muzzle; pull tight on the top of the nose and tie a single knot. Next, take the loose ends of the gauze and tie a single knot under the jaw. Bring the long ends of the gauze behind the ears and tie in a square knot or easy-to-release bow. Keep scissors handy to remove the muzzle in case the dog has trouble breathing.

"You don't want them to have trouble breathing. That can make things a lot worse," Dr. Ross says.

Choking

Signs of choking include excessive pawing at the mouth, blue lips, blue tongue, and gagging.

Force open your dog's mouth and look for a foreign object in the throat. If the animal will cooperate without biting you, grasp and remove the object by using tweezers or pliers. If the dog isn't cooperating and can at least partially breathe, hurry to a veterinarian.

If the item is lodged too deeply to reach or if your dog collapses, place your hands on both sides of the rib cage and apply firm, quick pressure. Alternatively, lay the pet on his or her side; using the palm of your hand, strike the rib cage firmly four times. Repeat the process until—hopefully—the item becomes dislodged. Contact a veterinarian right away.

First Aid Kit

*You can put together your own first aid kit or buy one from a pet store. The American Red Cross in many states offers pet first aid courses; to find a course near you, call your local Red Cross chapter or see **www.redcross.org/ services/hss/courses/pfachapter.html**. First aid kit contents can vary; your veterinarian may suggest items in addition to these:*

■ *gauze roll to wrap wounds or use as a muzzle*

■ *adhesive tape for bandages*

■ *nonstick bandages, such as Telfa pads*

■ *towels and cloth*

- milk of magnesia or activated charcoal to absorb poison. Use only with the advice of a veterinarian or poison control center before inducing vomiting or treating for poisoning with these products.

- eyedropper for oral treatments

- stretcher, such as a blanket, board or floor mat

- thermometer; a dog's normal temperature is 100 to 102.5 degrees

- tweezers

- antibiotic ointment

- cotton swabs

- instant cold pack

- first aid book

- scissors

- pliers to remove porcupine twills

- rags or rubber tubing for a tourniquet in life-threatening situations only

- Emergency phone numbers, including those of your veterinarian; an emergency animal hospital; and the ASPCA Animal Poison Control Center, which is (800) 548-2423. The center charges a forty-five-dollar fee. Its staff includes twenty-five veterinarians and five board-certified veterinary toxicologists.

Diarrhea

If your dog has diarrhea, you must determine the cause, not simply treat the symptom. "It is very important to keep in mind that there are many potential causes of diarrhea, some of them minor, others serious," says Richard Timmins, director of the Center for Animals in Society at the School of Veterinary Medicine at the University of California at Davis.

Common causes include parasites or eating garbage, a toy, food wrapper, toxin or gastrointestinal irritant. An abrupt change in diet can lead to diarrhea, as can stress, viral or bacterial infection, and food hypersensitivity. So can inflammatory bowel disease, and liver, kidney and metabolic diseases.

If diarrhea is accompanied by loss of appetite, depression, abdominal pain or vomiting, the dog should see a veterinarian. If the diarrhea persists three days or other signs develop, see a veterinarian.

Consider any changes in the dog's environment within the last twenty-four hours. Were pesticides, fertilizers, or herbicides sprayed where the dog could come into contact with them? Was he or she in a stressful situation? As long as the pet is adequately vaccinated, and is happy, alert, active, and otherwise behaving normally, Dr. Timmins says, owners can try these remedies for diarrhea. Do provide plenty of fresh water, as diarrhea can lead to dehydration.

Pectin/Kaolin

Administer a combination of pectin and kaolin, an antidiarrheal, at a dosage of two milliliters per kilogram (2.2 pounds) of the dog's body weight, three to four times daily. Figure that one milliliter equals a little less than one-quarter teaspoon. "There have been no studies confirming the effectiveness of this treatment," Dr. Timmins says, "but it is relatively safe."

Bismuth Salicylate

Bismuth salicylate may be used as an intestinal antiseptic at a dose of one to three milliliters per kilogram (2.2 pounds) of body weight daily, divided into three or four doses. The medication turns stools black, but the bismuth protects the gut mucosa and absorbs some bacterial toxins, Dr. Timmins says, adding: "Dogs don't find this medication to be particularly tasty."

To Feed or Not to Feed

If the problem is severe enough to consider withholding food, then the dog should see a veterinarian. Otherwise, feed the regular diet but divide it into three or four servings.

"There is some controversy about withholding food," Dr. Timmins says. "If the lining of the gut has been damaged, it will be unable to absorb nutrients, so the food particles will draw water into the gut, making the diarrhea worse. On the other hand, in order to repair itself, the cells lining the gut require energy, and production of that energy requires certain types of fermentable fiber found in the diet."

Very small or very young dogs shouldn't fast but should receive veterinary care, Dr. Rozanski says. "They will get dangerously low blood sugar if they don't eat frequently."

Lameness

Canine athletes and other active dogs may develop orthopedic soft tissue injuries. Signs of tearing or stretching of tendons, ligaments, and muscles include sudden lameness, pain, swelling, and refusal to bear weight on the affected limb. The injuries can occur with sudden twists and turns or from excessive use of muscles, tendons, and ligaments.

Just as human athletes are at higher risk for injury, so are athletic dogs participating in agility competitions, advanced obedience, or other active sports such as flyball, disc competitions, lure coursing, weight pulling, carting, sledding, and Schutzhund (a sport for working dogs). "Athletic dogs are going to be more prone to orthopedic injuries," Dr. Berg says.

Active sporting, hound and herding dogs, and others who participate in outdoor work or sports such as field trials, tracking, earth-dog competitions, and organized hunts can fall victim to these injuries.

"Strains and sprains are difficult to diagnose in dogs because they can't tell us where it hurts. But if we rule out any of the common causes of lameness that tend to be obvious in a physical exam, like cruciate ligament rupture, then we will do the same thing we do for people: prescribe rest," says Dr. Berg.

Gastritis

Most dogs experience an occasional bout of stomach upset.Their curiosity and sense of smell compel them to taste, chew, and swallow offending food or objects. As a result, they may develop gastritis, the most common stomach disorder that veterinarians see in otherwise healthy dogs. Especially prone are dogs who like to dine in the trash bin or longhaired ones who lick and swallow hair while grooming themselves.

"Gastritis simply refers to inflammation of the stomach," says

Mary Anna Labato, veterinary internist at Tufts.

If despite your best efforts, your dog gets into something he or she shouldn't, it may be comforting to know that acute gastritis usually disappears in less than a week. Chronic (long-term) gastritis arises from other causes and lasts longer, sometimes requiring lifelong care.

Gastritis affects male and female dogs equally. Young dogs tend to develop the acute form more often because they eat things they shouldn't, but dogs of all ages can develop the condition. The most common sign is vomiting. In that case, owners should withhold food and water until contacting a veterinarian. The vomiting may be mild or debilitating or even life threatening if it results in severe dehydration.

Not all vomiting is linked with gastritis; it may be regurgitation, the backward flow of food and fluid from the esophagus, minus stomach irritation. Or both acute and chronic gastritis can be associated with systemic diseases such as hypoadrenocorticism and diabetes mellitus. Numerous other disorders can be associated with vomiting, and many of them require a veterinarian's assistance to resolve.

Ear Problems

Owners should be alert to their dog's head-shaking and ear-scratching, signs of possible infection. "You may not be able to see everything going on inside the ear, but don't let that stop you," says Gene Nesbitt, Tufts clinical professor and consulting dermatologist with Tufts Dermatology and Allergy Service. "The bottom line is to get things checked out by a vet right away and to avoid letting the problem go on and on."

Trying to get a good look inside your dog's ears can ignite a battle of wills if the animal prefers petting and playing to poking and prodding. Alice Moon-Fanelli, a certified applied animal behaviorist at Tufts, stresses it's important to start early.

"Ideally, dogs should be desensitized to handling beginning when they are young puppies," she says. "Owners should pay particular attention to stroking the ears and paws and pair the handling with a positive experience. Click and treat training is an ideal method to desensitize adult dogs to accept and enjoy handling for examination and treatment."

Once your dog is accustomed to being examined, you'll discover that without an otoscope—a tool to check the ear's interior—you can see only the outer part. However, if problems exist there, they may indicate an internal ear problem requiring prompt veterinary attention.

"The main things people at home are going to find are odor, redness and a discharge or accumulation of debris on the inside of the ear flap," Dr. Nesbitt says. "These are all the results of underlying conditions. One of the most common problems is yeast and bacteria, or both and, if they go unattended, you'll get an infection. That causes more wax production and provides a medium for the creation of even more yeast and bacteria."

Ear mites, parasitic insects, are another cause for concern. Young dogs in group settings, such as shelters and pet stores, are more likely to have this problem than adults. Frontline or Revolution, ordinarily applied for fleas and ticks, can be an effective treatment treatment when used with a mitacide to kill mites in the ear canal.

If an examination shows only a small amount of wax, you can do the cleaning yourself, Dr. Nesbitt says. No method or tool works better than others, but take care to make sure you don't injure your dog.

"Some dogs have a lot of cracks and crevices at the base of the ear, so a Q-tip would be helpful in that area," he says. "Otherwise, it's not recommended that an owner use it to clean deep inside the ear because, if there is any debris in there, you'll just cram it down further. A good rule of thumb is to not try and clean something you can't see."

Numerous over-the-counter products are intended for ear maintenance. If you want to keep things simple, alcohol is a good solvent. Dr. Nesbitt advises using it only on the inside of the earflap. Otherwise, it can be an irritant.

Dogs with a lot of hair on the inside the ears, like Poodles, often require more work. Experienced owners can pluck the hair with tweezers or by hand, but Dr. Nesbitt suggests that most people leave this to professionals. "Groomers or veterinarians are better equipped to handle a situation like this," he says. "When using tweezers in a dog's ears, you can very easily do more harm than good."

When in Doubt

Dr. Berg encourages all pet owners to seek veterinary advice if they have any doubts about the seriousness of a soft tissue injury, especially after trauma. Sometimes related injuries are obvious, such as when a bone protrudes from the skin in a compound fracture. But more often, internal injuries aren't obvious.

"Some things that can be easily missed if an injured dog doesn't see a vet or if we don't look thoroughly enough are injuries inside the chest cavity, lungs, broken bones, spinal injury or other neurological damage," he says.

The bottom line: "The message for owners is that even though a bite wound or other soft tissue injury may not really look like much on the surface, it's possible that the trauma underneath is much worse," Dr. Berg says.

Finish That Medicine!

Don't assume a dog on antibiotics won't get an infected wound. Open wounds, especially when not properly cleaned and disinfected, can be resistant to antibiotics. Give your dog all the medication a veterinarian prescribes even if the wound seems healed.

About Car Accidents

"Dogs getting hit by cars is the single most common cause of trauma resulting in soft tissue injury," Tufts' Dr. John Berg says.

Car accidents often involve messy abrasions with significant skin loss. "Animals hit by cars can have quite a bit of skin loss with road debris in the wounds and in those cases, as with other wounds, preventing infection is our biggest concern," he says.

Dogs with major abrasions typically are sedated so that their wounds can be thoroughly cleaned and bandaged. "We sometimes watch them for a few days to make sure the wound is beginning to heal before we close it," Dr. Berg says. This delayed closure is called second intention closure and in some cases may require reconstructive techniques like skin grafts after healing begins.

If your dog is struck by a car, your veterinarian's primary concern will be any internal injuries that have damaged the respiratory system. One possible respiratory soft tissue injury is diaphragmatic hernia.

"The diaphragm is the sheet of muscle separating the chest from the abdomen and plays an important role in breathing," Dr. Berg says. "If that muscle gets a tear in it, abdominal contents can actually move through the tear into the chest cavity and cause significant breathing problems," Dr. Berg says. "This hernia can be fatal due to respiratory difficulty, or the dog might recover from the acute hernia but down the road, the hernia could completely close and obstruct the intestines" and surgery then would be needed.

Signs that a dog may have internal soft tissue injuries to the respiratory system include labored or rapid and shallow breathing, but sometimes the animal may not show any symptoms initially. "Lack of these signs doesn't mean there isn't a problem, especially after a trauma," Dr. Berg says. ■

Section II

Grooming

14

Hygiene Habits

Although all dogs develop their own unique grooming repertoire, most lick and nibble, shake and scratch, rub and roll.

To keep our canine pals looking their best, many of us regularly groom them. But no matter how good a job we think we're doing, our pals are oblivious to our efforts and continue with their own grooming routine. Your dog's efforts aren't necessarily geared toward improving his or her looks, however. Scientists suspect that in the wild, dogs groom to increase their chances of survival by keeping their coat clean and free of parasites and bacteria.

A Dog's Guide to Grooming

Licking and Nibbling

Your dog uses his or her tongue and teeth to tackle most grooming needs. Dogs lick to clean their coat and their anogenital area. Coat licking also seems to comfort dogs. "It's not unusual for a dog to almost go into a reverie when it's licking," observes Dr. Bruce Fogle, a London-based veterinarian. Dogs will often absent-mindedly stop in midlick—with the tongue on the body—then suddenly remember what they were doing and resume licking.

Dogs nibble themselves with their small front teeth (incisors) to relieve an itch, dislodge a burr, or remove matted hair. Long-haired canines often nibble at irritating matted hair between their toes.

Shaking when wet is a favorite canine pastime, but many dogs also shake after a nap or after they've been handled, presumably to restore their hair to its proper position

Shaking and Scratching

Shaking is the simplest grooming technique dogs use, and scratching is one of the most common. Most owners have witnessed (or been soaked by) the water-strewing, full-body shake that dogs delight in after a bath or swim. And scratching is a ubiquitous canine pastime. Many dogs scratch their forequarters with their hind toenails to relieve itchiness.

Rubbing and Rolling

While dogs usually rub to relieve an itch, some "highly evolved" house dogs have another reason for rubbing. "After a dog has finished its food, it will rub its face along the sofa due south, then due north," notes Dr. Fogle. As mystifying as it may seem, some experts suspect that "sofa rubbing" is simply your dog's method of wiping its mouth after a meal.

Rolling comes in two varieties: itch-relieving and scent-immersing. A dog will often roll to scratch an area on his or her back. But dogs also roll in foul-smelling, decomposing material, such as manure or garbage, to cover themselves with the scent. Scientists have come up with various theories to explain the purpose of this type of rolling. The "perfume" may serve to mask a dog's own scent so the animal can sneak up on prey; or it may be a way of attracting the attention of other dogs; or the odor may simply appeal to dogs.

Grooming Gone Awry

Since every dog develops characteristic grooming habits, owners need to know what's normal for their pet. Any change can signal a developing problem, and a close inspection is in order.

Irritant Grooming

If you notice your dog grooming a particular spot more often than usual, check for fleas (or other external parasites), a burr, or a mat of hair. If you discover fleas, talk to your veterinarian about the latest flea-control products. Fleas can cause your dog to lick or nibble a particular spot over and over, creating a "hot spot." If you discover a burr or matted hair, carefully remove the irritant and check the animal's skin for damage. If the skin appears irritated but you can't find a cause, the animal could have a bacterial skin infection. Excessively licking one spot can also indicate localized pain (from arthritis, for example). Have your veterinarian examine your pet to root out the cause of its overzealous grooming.

Compulsive Grooming

After a thorough examination, your veterinarian may conclude that your dog's excessive grooming isn't due to a medical ailment at all but is instead a compulsive behavior.

"Dogs with anxious or hyperactive temperaments tend to be predisposed to grooming disorders," explains Dr. Nicholas Dodman, director of the Behavior Clinic at Tufts University School of Veterinary Medicine. For these dogs, a moderate amount of stress (sometimes stemming from boredom or from restrictions on activity) can trigger a grooming compulsion. But—given enough stress—any dog can develop an "excessive grooming habit," with licking the most common manifestation.

"A dog will start to lick itself when it's bored or has its goals frustrated," says Dr. Dodman. But licking may become an entrenched habit, occurring even when the dog isn't under stress. Compulsive licking can be so relentless that the animal licks off its hair and damages the underlying skin, creating an ulcerated sore (lick granuloma). Some dogs—particularly small ones—compulsively groom between their toes or chew their toenails excessively.

Compulsion Control

While preventing compulsive disorders is easier than treating them, the techniques for both are the same. You need to eliminate as much stress as possible from your dog's daily life and then—since stress reduction often isn't enough—you'll need to increase the animal's exercise, evaluate his or her diet, and provide chew toys to keep the animal busy. Exercise spurs the release of brain chemicals that make a dog feel good and stabilize its mood. A diet lower in energy may help decrease your dog's excitability. And lots of safe chew toys— especially ones you can hide treats inside—will help keep your pet busy when you aren't around. "You want as much of your dog's day occupied with wonderful things as possible," says Dr. Dodman.

Unfortunately, some cases of compulsive grooming are so entrenched that making the above changes won't cure the disorder. In such cases, your veterinarian may prescribe an antiobsessional medication to help your dog overcome the compulsion. ■

15

Grooming

Primary reasons for grooming dogs are health and cleanliness. Here's how to make it an enjoyable experience for both of you.

From toenails to teeth to tail, grooming your dog is an intimate, personal issue. We groom our canine companions for their health and cleanliness and the satisfaction of seeing them look their best. However, "best" is a relative term and whatever it means to you, it can be difficult to achieve when something is amiss in the canine/human relationship. Precisely because grooming is such an intimate act, the process can invoke physical pain (an aching back, for instance), as well as feelings of impatience, frustration, and guilt in both you and your dog.

Forget Quick Fixes

Having a negative attitude about grooming your dog sends the wrong message and can damage your relationship with your pet. If you are stressed out and uncomfortable about the process, your dog likely will be too.

Attempts to groom under these circumstances can not only exacerbate a problem, but set up a mutually damaging cycle: the more your dog resists the process, the more you'll dislike grooming him or her. The more you shirk this duty, the more likely the animal will develop some of the very conditions grooming helps to prevent.

The primary reasons for grooming your dog are health and cleanliness. One benefit is that skin conditions, lumps, and injuries can be noticed and treated by you, or by a veterinarian if necessary. Neglecting to groom your dog can cause skin problems and pain from dirty and matted fur.

Positive Vibrations

If you're not grooming your dog on a regular basis, you and your dog can break the cycle and get back in harmony by working to change each other's perceptions about grooming. As the groomer, you are responsible for your dog's experience. In order to bring about a more perfect union of trust, harmony, and balance, you need to take the first step.

Begin by remembering when you and your dog shared a wonderful moment of complete trust, companionship, and harmony. Then try to maintain that feeling while you imagine grooming your dog. It may seem impossible to have those feelings during a grooming session, but read on! It's not just possible—it can even be fun!

Touching With Love

Grooming is based on touch more than anything else we do with and to our dogs. It's impossible to accomplish any of it without touching your dog, whether it's toenail trimming or tooth-brushing, flea combing or untangling matted fur, a quick lick and a promise or a laborious show "do." No matter how you define it, feel about it, or do it, grooming is a non-verbal form of communication that is transmitted through touch.

Helen Keller expressed this wonderfully: "I have just touched my dog. He was rolling on the grass with pleasure in every muscle and limb. I wanted to catch a picture of him in my fingers, and I touched him as lightly as I would a cobweb ... He pressed close to me, as if he were fain to crowd himself into my hand ... if he could speak, I believe he would say with me that paradise is attained by touch, for in touch is all love and intelligence."

To groom your dog with the touch of love and intelligence, to "catch a picture" of the animal in your fingers through touch. What you say and do with the animal and how you "listen" to what he or she is doing creates a feedback loop that results in an ever-more-meaningful and expansive conversation that replaces the old cycle of irritation, pain, and mistrust. Being willing to change our attitudes and approaches to grooming, and to help our dogs become cooperative participants, is a great start toward creating a rewarding ritual rather than a habitual pattern of balk/pull, whine/admonish, cower/encourage, yea/whew!

Brushing

Long, slow strokes over the whole body can calm and prepare a dog for grooming. If the animal is very nervous, use the back of the hand, a gently curled fist, or a fleece polishing glove to soften the contact.

■ A sewing seamer and thread cutter works well to separate and cut mats.

■ Use brushes with rounded tips to protect sensitive skin. Think about recreating a beauty parlor when brushing! Try humming or singing to establish a relaxing rhythm.

■ Specialized grooming tools are helpful, but not always necessary. If you can't find a comb, you can use a fork for working out mats; baking soda on a damp sponge for reducing odors; and petroleum jelly or vegetable oil for gooey things like tar.

■ Use round tipped-scissors to cut mats or tangles without cutting the skin. Use a comb between the skin and the mat to protect the skin from pointy scissors. Cornstarch, vegetable oil, or conditioner can be used on mats to soften and make them easier to comb out.

dematting comb

coarse dematter

shedding blade

rake

hard slicker

pin brush

Types of Brushes

The type of brush you use on your dog depends on the animal's hair-coat. A shedding blade—a long, flat blade doubled back into a loop, serrated on one side, flat on the other—can work wonders on thicker-coated dogs. The hard slicker's closely spaced, bent tines are designed to pull dead hair from the bottom layers of troublesome multiple coats. Rakes work like combs, except that the teeth are perpendicular to the handle and spaced wider apart.

A wire comb and slicker make a good combination for dogs with multiple coats like Shelties, says former groomer and veterinary technician Sandy Chow, now outreach coordinator for companion animals at the Humane Society of the United States.

"You want to get down to the skin," she says. "That's where the mats originate. Be careful, though, not to give a rash or burn."

For shedding machines like Huskies, Chow recommends regular brushing and use of a shedding blade. Its serrated edge catches dead hair and pulls it off the skin.

Some dogs, like Maltese, have a silkier coat and can feel the bite of blades and sharp brushes. A soft bristle brush or wire-tooth comb works best on their coats. Use a slicker with discretion, however, Chow says. Test it on your own skin to determine how much pressure to apply.

Avoid gimmicky brushes or shampoos that promise to get rid your

Use a wide-toothed comb or pick on mats or thick fur and start from the ends and work toward the skin. A comb with rotating teeth works well in sensitive areas such as behind the ears or on dogs who have very fine or thick tangled hair. Use round-tipped scissors for mats that can't be combed out easily.

dog of odor, she says. If your dog smells bad, it could be a sign of infection or other health problem, and a trip to the veterinarian may be in order.

Shedding

Many different factors influence the hair growth cycle, including ambient temperature and the photoperiod light exposure), nutrition, hormones, general state of health, genetics and growth, according to Dr. Gene Nesbitt, consulting dermatologist for Tufts Dermatology and Allergy Service.

"Hyperexcitable or nervous animals seem to shed more than calm ones," Dr. Nesbitt says. If the hair from large areas of the skin can be pulled easily, creating a bald spot), either hormonal problems, such as hypothyroidism or Cushing's disease, or follicular dysplasia (abnormal hair follicles) should be ruled out. If excessively shed hairs are not associated with patches of hair loss, the condition may cause inconvenience, but it is probably normal or at least causes no problem for the animal.

When there is no obvious clinical disease, you can try several things, Dr. Nesbitt says:

■ Modification of behavior or anti-anxiety treatments, especially if the dog is nervous or hyperexcitable.

■ Dietary modifications. Be sure the diet is well-balanced with adequate protein. If the skin is dry, try adding fatty acid supplementation.

■ Adjustment of light exposure. Decrease the length of exposure.

■ Adjustment of indoor temperature. Keep a lower temperature or keep your dog outside more often if it's cool.

"If no abnormal conditions can be discovered, or, if there is a poor response to the various changes, the only treatment is to remove the dead hairs from the animal by combing, brushing or possibly vacuuming," Dr. Nesbitt says.

Bathing

■ Place a towel on the living room floor and do everything you would do in the tub—without the water and shampoo. Go slowly and reward your dog often.

■ Lure the animal into the bathroom with treats, reward him or her, and let the dog go out again. To get your pet in the tub, put the treats on the rim, then on the bottom. Do several times in one day, then add turning on the sink water. Then put the treats at one end of the tub and turn the water on slowly at the other. Let the dog leave if he or she desires and gradually increase time and water amount.

■ For small, elderly, or arthritic dogs, use a stool or ramp to help them get in and out of a tub. Cover it and the tub bottom with non-skid material. Towels work well when wet. Dry their feet well if your floors are slippery.

■ Putting a soft visor on your dog's head will help keep soap and water out of his or her and ears.

■ If possible, put a small stool in the tub with your dog and sit on that; your back will thank you! Small dogs can be washed in the kitchen sink or on a table with two rubber tubs—one for washing, one for the final rinsing.

■ Keep your dog in the tub with peanut butter, cream cheese, or butter smeared on the end wall. For brushing, smear the food on the refrigerator or sprinkle treats on the floor.

Grooming by Necessity

Sometimes, your dog upsets your regular grooming schedule by getting into a sticky situation that requires immediate attention—you know, contact irritants such as gum, burrs, foxtails, or grease.

Above all, says Dr. Nesbitt, "don't use a solvent or anything like that. Many solvents are caustic and will cause contact irritation. I recommend a mild degreaser like Ivory or Dawn liquid dish soap. These are frequently used on birds in oil slicks."

Solvents such as turpentine and paint thinner can be dangerous. Beyond skin irritation, dogs are at risk of poisoning if they lick them on their skin. Use the liquid soap on sticky substances by squeezing it into your dog's hair. Gently rub it in to break up the substance and then rinse well. Be sure to keep the soap out of your dog's eyes.

If you can't remove the substance with liquid soap, you can try vegetable oil, but you have no guarantee the result will be other than a slippery dog with matted hair. In some circumstances, the only recourse is cut away the mats.

"Be careful!" warns Dr. Robin Downing, affiliate faculty member of Colorado State University College of Veterinary Medicine and Biomedical Sciences and owner of Windsor Animal Hospital in Colorado. "Always use a guarded clipper. We routinely get people who cut their dog's skin, and the dog needs suturing."

The moving blades of electronic, guarded clippers don't come in contact with skin. If you don't have one or know how to use one, contact the veterinarian or groomer to help remove the substance.

Here are instructions for removing substances in your dog's haircoat:

- ***Chewing gum:*** *Scissors are the most efficient, Dr. Nesbitt says. But take care not to cut the dog.*

- ***Water-soluble paint:*** *Wash with warm, soapy water and rinse.*

- ***Oil-based paint:*** *Clip it out. "Any solvents strong enough to remove the paint have a strong potential for causing an irritant reaction," Dr. Nesbitt says.*

- ***Tree sap, grease, oil:*** *Try an emulsifying liquid soap like Dawn and rinse well.*

- ***Tar:*** *Ask the veterinarian for advice on using guarded clippers.*

- ***Feces:*** *Gently comb out the excess. Bathe with a pH balanced shampoo and conditioner for dogs. Shampoos made for humans can irritate the haircoat.*

- ***Skunk smell or decaying animal odor:*** *Gently comb out the excess. Bathe with a dog shampoo and conditioner.*

- ***Sugar syrup:*** *Apply warm, soapy water to loosen it. Rub liquid soap on the mats. Rinse well and bathe.*

- ***Sand:*** *Brush out the excess and then bathe.*

■ *Dried salt water:* Bathe.

■ *Burrs and stickers:* Comb out those you can. If the hair has mats, use guarded clippers to remove the substance from hair.

■ *Foxtails (grass awns):* Comb out those you can. Search for foxtails buried in skin and seek veterinary assistance to remove them.

Nail Trimming

■ Trim nails frequently (every three to four weeks) and only remove a quarter inch or so to avoid cutting the quick.

■ For black nails, use a strong penlight to locate the quick.

■ Try diamond files for nail trimming. They come in a variety of shapes, materials and grits. Start with the finest grit and work up. File in the direction of the nail grain and gently hold the nail to minimize vibration and movement. Pumice stones also work well for nail shortening.

■ As an alternative to trimming the front nails, put sandpaper on the front and back door and teach your dog to scratch it when she wants to go out. Frequent walks on paved surfaces also can help keep nails short.

You'll find additional information on both bathing and nail trimming elsewhere in this book. ■

16

Lather Up!

Get the lowdown on how often your dog needs to be bathed, and what you need to know about the products to use.

D ogs in the wild don't need baths. Why do our dogs? Well, they don't need baths, but if they want to live in our homes, and sometimes even sleep in our beds, they have to look and smell cleaner than dogs normally do. Shampoos used to bathe your dog can be formulated for general cleaning, or for specific purposes, such as killing fleas or soothing irritated skin.

How Often Is Often Enough?

You hear all kinds of advice about how often you should bathe your dog. Some say once a month. Some say once a year. Some say even that's too frequent. What's the right answer?

It depends on the dog, the owner, and their lifestyles, says Dr. Gene Nesbitt, consulting dermatologist for Tufts Dermatology and Allergy Service. "It really has to be tailored to the individual dog," he says. Dr. Nesbitt says some dogs need to be bathed weekly or twice weekly to prevent a serious buildup of dandruff.

"The bottom line is that if you're bathing a dog for cosmetic reasons or routine odor control, you can bathe most of them with varying frequency and not have any problems," he says. "Bathing a dog is more often about troubleshooting. Is it for yeast or bacterial lesions? Do you have an itchy dog, and you're using shampoos to try and control the itching?"

Dr. Nesbitt notes that many medicated shampoos do have a tendency to remove some of the oiliness from the skin. "There's a normal lipid layer—fatty film on the surface—that holds moisture in," he says. "So if we're using these shampoos that are removing what we want, we may very well remove some of the protective layer and make them more susceptible to dry skin or another problem."

---

66 BATHING A DOG IS OFTEN

ABOUT TROUBLESHOOTING. IS IT

FOR YEAST OR BACTERIAL LESIONS?

DO YOU HAVE AN ITCHY DOG? 99

Getting Started

If no skin issues are involved, almost anything will work in terms of bathing, Dr. Nesbitt says. However, if skin problems exist, they have to be addressed on an individual basis. "This is where the veterinarian's knowledge and input come into play," he says.

"If you have an itchy dog, we suggest bathing in cool water. If your dog doesn't have this kind of problem, then warm water is fine," Dr. Nesbitt says.

He recommends being especially careful to keep the shampoo out of the dog's eyes. "I recommend an ointment over eyes drops for this because liquids can't form the same kind of protective barrier that oil-based ointments do," Dr. Nesbitt says. An ointment puts a film over the cornea so you don't have direct contact between any irritant and the eye. This is an especially important precaution when bathing for medical purposes, and you're treating a specific area around the head and muzzle." It is not necessary to put cotton balls in your dog's ears during bathing to keep out water.

The type of shampoo you use depends on why you're bathing. Dogs with dandruff can benefit from shampoos formulated for that purpose; if your dog has a fungal or parasite problem, your veterinarian can recommend special shampoos. "If you've just got an itchy dog with no buildup, generally the shampoos are oatmeal-based," Dr. Nesbitt says.

It's important to use an appropriate shampoo so that the dog's coat doesn't become dried out unnecessarily. "Some shampoos are a little harsh if they're being used when they're not needed, like strong degreasers," Dr. Nesbitt says. "In those cases, then you'll have even more dryness."

He also recommends using a conditioner after rinsing the dog. "The majority are either oatmeal or aloe based and are fairly mild," he says. "There again, if you're treating for some specific reason, select your conditioner based on what you're trying to accomplish."

How to Dry

If your dog has skin problems, toweling may be the proper drying option.

Drying a dog after a bath is another topic about which dog owners are divided. Some owners say blow-dryers can burn dogs; others swear by the dryers. Who is right?

"A lot of dogs are dried with hair dryers at groomers," Dr. Nesbitt says. "Long hair can take a lot of time to comb out and dry if you use a towel."

He adds: "The advantage of the blow-drying is that it keeps the hair from tangling and makes brushing much more manageable. A groomer routinely does this because it gives more fluffiness to the hair."

However, he notes, "if you have a dog that is itchy, it can aggravate that condition. It also will add to the troubles of a dog with pre-existing dry skin and dandruff problems. These are the dogs to towel dry."

Bathe Without Water

These days, it's possible to clean your dog without a drop of water, thanks to dry, or rinseless, shampoo. These shampoos aren't really dry except for the powder variety, but they're called dry because they don't require water.

You can spot-clean with these products (if, for instance, your dog is dirty only on one part of his or her body), or you can clean the entire dog. Dry shampoos can be a good option for canines who hate water and baths and for senior dogs who aren't up to a full bath. They're also practical for dogs who may be vomiting or who have diarrhea and can't handle frequent baths as well as for dogs recuperating from surgery with incisions that must remain dry.

Do keep in mind that rinseless shampoos don't replace a water and shampoo bath. With these products, your dog won't feel as clean and will get dirty again faster than if he or she had had a regular bath. Consider these products as stopgaps. You'll find them in powder, spray or foam form.

Reading the Fine Print

You can learn so much from reading labels, but the manufacturers of cosmetic products (human and canine) are often reluctant to give their consumers too much information, perhaps because most products are more similar than their makers like to admit.

Sometimes the only differences between an expensive shampoo and an inexpensive one are the last few ingredients—which means there is very little difference between them at all.

Contents are required to be listed on the label in descending order of their presence in the product, until you get to the substances that represent less than one percent of the mixture; then they may be listed in any order at all. Since shampoos are usually about 70 to 90 percent water, by the time you get to the preservative or fragrance ingredients (often midway through the list), each substance listed comprises less than one percent of the total content—a minute quantity, and not enough to make an appreciable difference to the effectiveness of the shampoo.

Don't be discouraged if you see long, impossible-to-pronounce chemicals when you look at ingredients lists. While long names are often an indication of unhealthy substances in food products, they are the norm in cosmetic ingredients. In fact, by referring to the list below, which identifies the most common safe ingredients found in shampoo, grouped according to their function, you can easily confirm the purpose and safety of every ingredient in the bottle.

Cleansing Agents
All shampoos contain one or more of these cleansing agents. These help remove dirt and oil from the hair and skin.

Ammonium laureth sulfate; ammonium lauryl sulfate; cococamphodiacetate; cocamidopropyl betaine; sodium cocoglyceryl ether sulfonate; sodium laureth sulfate; sodium lauryl sarcosinate; sodium lauryl sulfate.

Lathering Agents

These ingredients are added to shampoos to create lather. Contrary to popular belief, lather does not actually clean the hair. The physical process of building and then rinsing away the lather, however, helps distribute the cleansing agents evenly around the hair. As a rule, people feel better about shampoos that create a lot of lather, but it's strictly a psychological advantage.

Interestingly, the amount of lather you get while shampooing is affected by the amount of oil and debris in the fur. The cleaner the hair, the more lather you will get when using the shampoo. Some shampoo makers instruct their users to shampoo twice; if you do, you'll notice the lather increases on the second round.

Cocamide MEA; luramide MEA; lauric DEA; polysorbate-20.

Conditioners

These agents moisturize the hair, make it easy to comb, and smoother to the touch.

Amino acids; collagen; panthenol; protein.

Humectants

Humectants are agents in shampoos that attract and hold water in the hair, making it feel full, soft, and thick.

Glycerin; glycols; glycosphingolipids; hyaluronic acid; mucupolysaccharides; sodium PCA; sorbitol.

Quaternary Ammonium Compounds

These ingredients give hair a slick feel.

Behenalkonium betaine; behentrimonium chloride; benzalkonium chloride; cetrimonium chloride; dicetydimonium chloride; quaternium-18; stearalkonium chloride.

Thickeners

These ingredients are responsible for the shampoo's thickness:

Caprylic acid; cetyl alcohol; glycol stearate; hydrogenated lanolin; palmitic acid; PEGs; stearyl alcohol.

Preservatives

These agents are crucial to the shampoo because they help keep contamination of the many ingredients to a minimum.

Methylparaben; phenoxyethanol; propylparaben; quaternium 15.

Tub Alternatives

In mild weather, bathing your dog outside with a garden hose is one alternative—if he or she doesn't mind cold water. But many temperature-sensitive canines won't tolerate such treatment. And in winter, owners in many parts of the country don't have this option.

So what's the owner of a dirty dog to do? You can take advantage of the "dog washes" sponsored by local humane societies or animal shelters and support two good causes at once—your dog's hygiene and the welfare of homeless dogs. But these events don't always coincide with your dog's latest roll in something raunchy.

Taking your dog to a groomer can be a convenient alternative, but you still have to spend time finding a reputable groomer with the proper equipment and facilities. Some dogs don't take kindly to handling by strangers, so factor in your dog's temperament when you consider whether to hire a groomer. The advent of mobile dog-grooming vans and pick-up/drop-off services has expanded the options and largely eliminated the logistical hassles, but you usually pay a premium for such convenience.

Self-service dog-wash parlors, a growing trend in some parts of the country, have the advantages of equipment specifically designed for bathing dogs and do-it-yourself cost savings. The best of these facilities offer sanitized, ergonomically positioned tubs with humane restraint devices; no-slip flooring; water delivered at a safe pressure and temperature; no-clog drains; grooming tables with dryers; and well-trained staff to help novices get started.

The Skinny on "Natural" Skin-Care Products

When faced with the abundance of dog shampoo and skin-care products offered in pet stores and catalogs, many people opt for so-called "natural" products, believing they are inherently better than their synthetic counterparts. But "natural" is not necessarily synonymous with "nontoxic." There is no product, natural or synthetic, to which some animals won't react adversely.

Many natural shampoos and skin-care products contain oils distilled from pennyroyal, citrus fruit, and the Australian melaleuca tree. When used as directed, these ingredients may help repel (and even kill) parasitic insects and heal minor skin irritations or infections. But these oils can be absorbed through a dog's skin and, if overused, can cause toxic reactions ranging from severe skin inflammation and excessive salivation to loss of muscle coordination and seizures.

The fact that natural shampoos and skin-care products are not regulated by the U.S. Food and Drug Administration or the Environmental Protection Agency may not mean they're less safe than synthetic products, but it does mean they're not required to be as thoroughly tested. Sometimes, the actual concentrations of active ingredients are not listed on the product labels, and without regulatory oversight, quality control during manufacturing may be compromised. Moreover, if health problems arise with nonregulated natural products, manufacturers are not obligated to inform consumers about these problems.

If your dog shows any sign of an adverse reaction within two to eight hours after bathing or the application of any skin-care product, contact your veterinarian. Better yet, to avoid such a scenario, before you use any "natural" shampoo or skin-care product that's not labeled to your satisfaction, call the manufacturer for a complete list of ingredients and their concentrations. (If the manufacturer doesn't answer your questions satisfactorily, don't use the product.) Then ask your veterinarian if those constituents and amounts are likely to harm your dog.

Also, if any product looks or smells "off," don't use it. If improperly stored, some aromatic oils can degrade into harmful turpentine-like compounds. Finally, whether you use natural or synthetic products, always read the label and follow usage directions. If those directions include rinsing, be sure to rinse your dog thoroughly. ■

17

Clean Teeth—
The First Defense

*Keeping your dog's teeth clean is critical; here's how
to do it yourself. And, check out the medical advances
for helping dogs with serious dental problems.*

At some time or another, every dog lover has endured a blast of bad breath from an ardent canine companion. Indeed, foul-smelling breath is so prevalent among dogs that the very phrase has come to be an insult, as in, "Get lost, dog breath!"

Even so, a mention of the idea of preventive dental hygiene for dogs strikes some people as weird, if not nearly ridiculous. "Toothbrushes for dogs? You've got to be kidding!"

But it's no joke. Chew on these findings: a University of Minnesota epidemiology study of sixty-seven thousand dogs and cats showed oral disease to be the most common canine and feline clinical disease. And a Kansas State University study showed periodontal disease to be associated with chronic internal organ diseases of the heart, kidneys, and liver. Surprisingly, dental problems rank as the No. 1 disease among pets.

Our own dog husbandry practices are to blame for most of the factors that contribute to the poor condition of our dogs' teeth—including the diets that we provide for our dogs and human-engineered breeding programs.

Fortunately, this means that dog owners also have the power to reverse this unhealthy trend: You can observe your pet's teeth for early signs of trouble, enabling you to treat small problems before they worsen; you can give your dogs nutritional support for healthy teeth and gums; and you can help keep their teeth clean. By implementing a thoughtful plan for dental health, you can help ensure your dog's teeth will contribute to his longevity and zest for life and keep his or her "kisses" fresher.

Clean Teeth = Good Health

The focus of all dental care is the removal of plaque—which is composed of a mixture of oral bacteria, bacterial sugars, salivary proteins, and food and cellular debris—and dental calculus or tartar—which is comprised of a mixture of mineralized concretions of salivary calcium and phosphate salts. The presence of plaque on the teeth can cause gum inflammation or gingivitis, visible as a reddening of the tissue along the gum line. (Tartar does not directly cause gingivitis; rather, the calculus serves as a spot for plaque to collect and for bacteria to multiply.)

With dogs, "cavities" in the teeth are rare; it's gingivitis that wreaks havoc with the dog's health. Initially, it's the pain of gingivitis that diminishes the dog's quality of life; not only do dogs use their mouths for eating or drinking, but also for grooming, social interaction, and playing with toys. If a dog is reluctant to use his or mouth for any of these activities, the gum problems can worsen due to reduced circulation.

If the gingivitis advances to a full-blown periodontal infection, it can make the dog very sick. "One single infected root can make a dog—or a person, for that matter—seriously ill," warns Dr. Nancy Scanlan, a veterinarian with a holistic practice in Sherman Oaks, California. "And oral infection can constantly enter your bloodstream and cause trouble elsewhere in the body. It can wreak havoc with the joints, lungs, kidneys, liver ... you can get into multiple body problems from one little tooth."

Dog Breath Isn't Funny

Halitosis can be a harbinger of serious disease, most likely periodontal disease, an inflammation or infection of the gums and the teeth's supporting tissues.

"Bad dog breath could also be a sign of an oral tumor, kidney disease and, in acute cases, diabetic ketoacidosism," a buildup of ketones or fat cells in diabetes mellitus that is considered a medical emergency, says Bonnie Shope, an assistant clinical professor with a special interest in dentistry at Tufts University School of Veterinary Medicine.

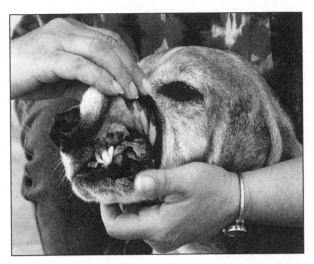

This older dog displays the classic effects of long-term dental neglect: tartar-encrusted teeth and resultant gingivitis.

Dogs with diabetic ketoacidosis could have breath resembling acetone. Dogs with kidney failure could smell excessively sweet or ammonia-like. Whatever their odor, dogs with any bad breath should have an oral exam by a veterinarian. "Usually, it means that they need a dental cleaning and possibly could have more advanced dental disease necessitating additional treatment—root planing [removal of plaque and tartar below the gum line], extractions or root canals," Dr. Shope says.

No studies are available on the effectiveness of teeth-cleaning products such as sprays, liquids to add to the dog's water, and mints to freshen the breath.

Man-Made Problem

No one is likely to verify this firsthand, but wild canines, like wolves and coyotes, are unlikely to share domesticated dogs' dental problems, in large part because our dogs don't use their teeth in the same way as their wild brethren. The sharp front teeth of dogs are designed for cutting through tissue and tearing raw meat; the powerful jaws and sturdy back teeth are best used for gnawing on and crushing bones. Wild canines who engage in these activities daily generally have strong teeth that are scraped clean, with healthy gums.

But the efficient design of the dog's teeth is wasted on our domestic pets, who usually eat kibble or canned food. Dog teeth were never intended to chew foods like these. (Ironically, it's we humans, who have teeth that are ideally suited for chewing nuggets of dry dog food—grinding teeth with flattened tops.) Canned and soft food are even worse for dogs' teeth; they lack even the minimal abrasive action provided by dry food, and are more likely to contain sugars that contribute to dental disease.

Humans have also expedited their dogs' dental problems through hundreds of generations of breeding to create a tremendous variety in the shape and size of dogs, especially in the canine head. Unique characteristics have been refined in different breeds over time. Most dogs still have forty-two permanent teeth, regardless of size or shape of the jaw. But in many breeds, this has resulted in crowding of teeth, which can lead to increased retention of plaque, gingivitis (inflammation of the gums), and eventually, to loss of teeth and infection. Today, tooth extractions are routine in a multitude of breeds; without extractions, many dogs would be unable to survive the crowded, dysfunctional mouths they have inherited.

Four Easy Steps to Dental Health

Four out of five dogs show signs of oral disease by age three, according to the American Veterinary Dental Society. Want to protect your dog's teeth? Follow these tips:

- *Every six to twelve months, schedule a dental oral exam.*

- *Schedule professional dental cleanings as needed.*

- *Brush teeth daily. Brushing every other day doesn't maintain clinically healthy gums, the* Journal of Veterinary Dentistry *reported. If you must brush every other day, then also give your dog a dental hygiene chew. That will reduce plaque and gingivitis.*

- *Serve dog food and treats that have received the Veterinary Oral Health Council's official seal of approval for controlling tartar and/or plaque.*

Teeth Cleaning Controversies

Everyone agrees that dogs' teeth should be clean. But as soon as we begin to talk about ways to remove plaque from our dogs' teeth, arguments ensue. The people who maintain that by feeding our dogs

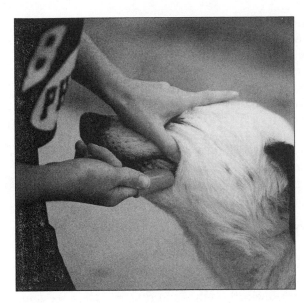

Brushing your dog's teeth takes practice, for you and your dog!

a diet that is as close to that of wild canines as possible (consisting largely of raw meat and bones), contend that dogs should be able to maintain clean teeth all on their own. Feeding a raw diet is time-consuming, expensive, and potentially dangerous to the dog. The diets are nutritionally incomplete, and dogs can die from ingesting bacteria in raw meat. These owners are more than happy to brush their dogs' teeth, if that's what is necessary to keep their dogs "safe" from the pitfalls of the raw food bones diets.

One truth that stands above the fray is that you don't have to stand by helplessly while sinister events are taking place in your dog's mouth. Obviously, there are advantages and disadvantages to every dental health approach. As always, you will have to choose the options that make the most sense for you and your dog.

Regular Dental Exams

That said, be aware that most veterinarians maintain that the first part of a good dental health program is professional evaluation. An oral exam should be an integral part of every veterinary checkup, starting from a puppy's earliest health examination. Your veterinarian will check your puppy's bite to make sure the teeth mesh well, and to monitor the loosening of his or her deciduous (or "baby") teeth and the eruption of permanent teeth.

Normally, in the process of shedding the deciduous teeth, the roots dissolve and the newly unmoored teeth fall out to make way for the permanent teeth. When these baby teeth are said to be "retained," it's because the roots have failed to dissolve normally. If a tooth is erupting awry, or the deciduous teeth are retained, your veterinarian will be able to judge whether or not to intercede with an extraction, or whether some method of orthodontia should be used to bring errant teeth to the appropriate place.

As your dog ages, your veterinarian will also be able to monitor the condition of any teeth your dog may have broken or worn down to the nub. These conditions don't always require treatment, but they must be observed for signs of infection or other problems.

Professional Cleaning

In addition to examinations, many veterinarians believe that dogs should have at least one annual prophylactic teeth cleaning to support all-around health—even though some dog owners have concerns about the anesthesia required for these procedures. In an effort to expose the dog to as few drugs as possible, as long as the examination showed that a dog's teeth were clean and white, some veterinarians would sanction passing up the annual cleaning. But given the number of serious health concerns that bad teeth can cause, other veterinarians make a case for a more aggressively preventative plan.

According to Edward Eisner of Veterinary Dental Service in Greenwood Village, Colorado, "Ideally, a dog should have its teeth cleaned within the first eighteen months of life. A perfect time to do this is while the dog is being anesthetized for spaying or neutering. Teeth cleaning visits should also include an educational session with the pet's owner, to teach toothbrushing."

During this initial educational visit, Dr. Eisner suggests that veterinarians gauge the owner's interest in home dental care. The suggested interval between teeth-cleaning visits, he says, will depend on the condition of the dog's mouth and the owner's interest in or ability to maintain the dog's clean teeth.

According to Dr. Eisner, a thorough cleaning will include ultrasonic scaling to remove plaque and calculus above and beneath the gum line, in addition to manual work with hand-held dental tools. Periodontal therapy, he says, goes a step beyond routine cleaning, by scaling the root surfaces. Finally, polishing the tooth surface is accomplished with a tiny, vibrating rubber cup and abrasive dentifrice to discourage plaque adherence.

One of the reasons these thorough cleanings are necessary, says

Eisner, is because dogs with periodontal disease may or may not exhibit problems. Their owners may report nonclinical signs of tooth problems, without recognizing them as such. These behaviors include poor self-grooming, incessant nose licking, hesitancy to open or close the mouth all the way, decreased chewing of toys or treats, pawing at the mouth, facial rubbing, head or mouth handling shyness, or a sudden preference for soft food. Other symptoms include bad breath, sneezing, and one-sided nasal discharge.

Owners of small dogs and older dogs need to devote more time and attention to their dogs' teeth, says Eisner, because these dogs have a much higher incidence of periodontal disease than do large or young dogs. "In a situation of chronic inflammation, the bone will shrink away from the gums at a rate of 1.5 millimeters per year. An Akita tooth may have a root 30 millimeter thick, a Chihuahua only 5 millimeter thick. At the rate of 1.5 millimeters per year of bone loss, the Akita has time before there is a noticeable problem, but the Chihuahua has only a couple of years before radical therapy is needed."

Bones

Chewing bones has two potential benefits for dogs: it helps keep their teeth clean and it can reduce boredom when they are alone. Although problems caused by chewing and swallowing bones are actually quite unusual, owners should remember that chewing bones is not a completely safe activity for dogs. In particular, small, irregularly shaped, rough-edged bones such as beef vertebrae can become lodged in the esophagus (the tube that carries food from the mouth to the stomach), causing life-threatening problems for dogs.

Bones almost always are dissolved in the digestive process, and very rarely cause problems. To avoid obstructing the esophagus, owners should offer their dogs large, hard bones such as beef ribs or leg bones. And remember, chewing bones is not a substitute for a regular program of dental care.

Chew Toys

Necessity is the mother of marketing; as a result, there are literally thousands of products advertised as beneficial to dogs' dental health. And there are also thousands of opinions about the dangers or virtues of each of these products.

Rope-based toys have gained popularity as "dog dental floss," and there are dozens of toys that incorporate knotted ropes into their designs: mint-scented ropes, ones that "crackle," ropes with plastic pieces that are meant to be chewed, and so on. As consumption of these products increases, increasing numbers of veterinarians are extracting rope and string from various parts of their patients' anatomy.

The same can be said of every other type of toy; most veterinarians have performed surgery on at least a few dogs with hunks of Nylabone, rawhide, Frisbee, or other toy materials impacted in their intestines.

Recommendations

We asked Eisner to help us formulate chew-toy recommendations.

■ His first caution is to use simple common sense: watch your dog when he or she is chewing on anything. "Supervision is required any time you give your dog something to put in his mouth."

■ Eisner recommends choosing chews that either soften as the dog chews them, or products that "give," but do not readily crack or split. One such toy is the Dental Kong, described by Eisner as "a terrific device, made of non-harmful materials, and resilient."

What about rawhide chews, or animal products, such as pig ears? "There is dental benefit to rawhide, but it's critical that you keep an eye out for little pieces coming off and being swallowed," Eisner says. "When rawhide toys get soft enough to start coming apart, they must be taken from the dog."

Delivering the Goods

Dentrifices are available in several delivery systems: toothpastes (which are generally scrubbed onto the teeth and gums), gels (topically applied to the gums), liquid rinses (which are squirted into the mouth), rawhide chews that have been impregnated with the substances, and small cloth pads (which are wiped onto the teeth and gums). In Eisner's estimation, the most effective are the toothpastes and the rawhide chews, because of the abrasive action they provide; the least helpful are the pads.

"If you think about your own teeth-cleaning experiences, it's easy to judge these different forms," he says. "The goal is to apply the dentifrice to as many surfaces of the teeth and gums as possible. One benefit of the liquids is that they readily wash into crevices and crannies in the dog's teeth and gums. But a shortcoming is that they provide no abrasive or scrubbing action; imagine only using mouth-

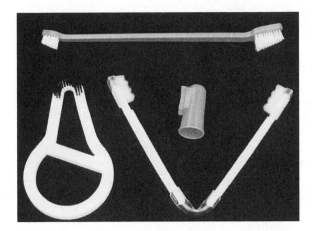

Test different brushes to find the one that works best for you.

wash, and never brushing your teeth."

Eisner finds the teeth-cleaning pads to be the least useful delivery system, since they can neither deliver the dentifrices to every surface of the dog's teeth or gums, nor scrub the teeth very efficiently.

D-I-Y Teeth Cleaning

While occasional professional cleaning is important, toothbrushing is the best way to remove plaque from the dog's teeth.

Some toy and brachycepalic breeds—those with pushed-in faces such as Pugs and Shih Tzus—may be prone to dental problems because of their anatomy, but the irrefutable truth is that good oral hygiene can prevent most of them. In two words: daily brushing.

If dogs are new to brushing, Dr. Shope recommends building up slowly over time. "Introduce it gradually, using positive reinforcement—treats and praise. Do it at the same time every day in the same place."

Any soft-bristled toothbrush may be used; it doesn't have to be a special brush for dogs, although several manufacturers have innovated brushes that can make the task marginally easier.

■ Brushes that are two-sided or have bristles arranged in a semicircle allow you to scrub both sides of a tooth at the same time.

■ Several manufacturers make rubber or plastic "fingertip" brushes that you slip on like the finger of a glove; they have bristles affixed to the tip.

■ One manufacturer makes a long-handled brush with a large head at one end and a small head at the other—great for long-nosed dogs and big dogs.

Canine Dental Glossary

- **Periodontal disease:** *refers to the inflammation of some of the tooth's support caused by bacteria that leads to plaque buildup on teeth and bone loss below the gum line.*

- **Occlusion:** *a normal bite for a dog. Refers to the alignment of the teeth.*

- **Malocclusion:** *an abnormal bite.*

- **Maxillary prognathism:** *informally known as an overbite, this condition occurs when the dog's upper jaw is longer than the lower jaw.*

- **Maxillary brachygnathism:** *informally called an underbite, this condition occurs when the dog's upper jaw is shorter than the lower jaw. Veterinary dentists can correct both overbites and underbite.*

- **Anondontia:** *missing teeth.*

- **Supernumerary:** *extra teeth. Adult dogs typically have forty-two teeth.*

- **Periapical granuloma:** *tooth abscess.*

- **Endodontic treatment:** *tooth canal treatment.*

The Value of Toothpaste

Toothpaste is not necessary to get the dog's teeth clean, though it can make the project easier. Don't use the stuff from your family's medicine cabinet, however. Human toothpastes can irritate dogs' intestinal tracts. Those containing fluoride can be toxic when swallowed excessively. Special meat- or peanut butter-flavored toothpastes for dogs have two advantages: they are far more attractive to dogs than minty "people" toothpastes, and they contain substances that are better suited to killing the bacteria found in dog mouths. "Let them initially lick the paste off the brush to enjoy the flavor,"

Dr. Shope says. "Concentrate brushing the outside surfaces of the teeth. Opening the mouth wide to get the side facing the tongue often makes dogs resistant."

Toothpastes can work two ways: mechanically and chemically. Some contain inert abrasive materials such as calcium or silicate, which take a significant mechanical role in helping scrub plaque and other matter from the teeth and gums. But even those pastes without abrasives can play a mechanical role, by lubricating the bristles of a toothbrush for better action.

> ❝ ...THE MOST EFFECTIVE ARE THE TOOTHPASTES AND THE RAWHIDE CHEWS, BECAUSE OF THE ABRASIVE ACTION THEY PROVIDE. ❞

Toothpastes can also work chemically. Today, a variety of substances are employed to kill the bacteria that lends itself to plaque formation. Two such substances are chlorhexidine and hypothiocyanate. The former kills the aerobic (oxygen-dependent) bacteria commonly found in a healthy dog mouth. The latter is aimed at killing the pathogenic (illness-causing) anaerobic bacteria that multiply in and "infect" periodontal pockets in an unhealthy dog mouth. Which type of product you use should depend on the condition of your dog's periodontal area (the gum/tooth margin). If the dog has tight, pink gums and teeth with little tartar, the chlorhexidine products are more appropriate. The hypothiocyanate products are helpful when the dog is known to have periodontal problems.

Diet and Dental Health

From your dog's dental-health perspective, anything that mechanically removes plaque—the sticky accumulation of bacteria, food particles, and saliva on teeth that precedes more serious dental disorders—is helpful. Thus, it's generally believed that eating dry dog food reduces the risk of gingivitis (gum inflammation) and periodontitis (severe inflammation and erosion of tissue surrounding the teeth).

But when it comes to attacking plaque, dry food can't hold a candle to regular tooth brushing. "If you brush your dog's teeth every day or two, it doesn't really matter what it eats," notes Dr. Cecilia Gorrel, a well-known veterinary dentist practicing in the U.K. Also, when brushing your dog's teeth, you're more likely to notice other oral anomalies, such as tooth fractures or early-stage tumors.

While hard, abrasive kibble can help clean your dog's teeth, "for dry food to effectively scrape the teeth, the dog has to chew the food, not swallow it whole," notes Dr. Laura LeVan, a veterinary dentist practicing in Massachusetts. Consequently, the size of the kibble and your dog's eating style will help determine dry food's plaque-removal power. Also be wary of teeth-cleaning claims made by manufacturers of crunchy dog treats. To get dental benefits from some of these, your dog may have to eat very large quantities of them.

Unfortunately, even if you brush your pet's teeth daily and feed him or her only dry food, tooth and gum problems still may develop. That's because the immune response to the bacteria in plaque varies dramatically from dog to dog. "I have seen dogs with massive plaque and tartar buildup and no periodontal disease and those with spotlessly clean mouths and severe periodontal disease," says Dr. Peter Kertesz, a veterinary dentist in the U.K. who also treats companion and zoo animals. Also, as a dog ages, his or her immune system weakens, making the animal more susceptible to the effects of periodontal bacteria.

While studies suggest that large dogs are less prone to periodontal disease than small dogs, individual genetic makeup largely determines a dog's susceptibility to the bacteria in plaque. So

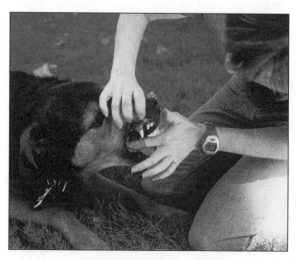

A weekly check of your dog's mouth can reveal dental problems early on.

generalizations about size and breed may be misleading. Assuming a dog receives appropriate dental care, perhaps the best indicator of the animal's prospects for "good teeth" is the oral health of his or her parents.

Root Canals for Dogs?

Your best efforts may not be able to prevent your dog from cracking a tooth. Depending on the severity of the crack, a veterinary dentists may recommend saving and strengthening the tooth through endodontic therapy, known colloquially as a root canal. Root canal is a misnomer; the process targets the tooth and has little or nothing to do with roots or canals.

The process is more common than a pet owner might think, particularly among dogs who devour rocks and gnaw cow hooves, says William Rosenblad, head of the department of oral surgery and dentistry at MSPCA Angell Memorial Animal Hospital in Boston, considered one of the world's foremost clinical veterinary institutions.

A study of military dogs, for instance, examined the health of the canine teeth of 142 dogs; one in four had at least one fractured canine tooth, typically due to attack exercises, abnormal chewing or abnormal biting behavior, the *Journal of Veterinary Dentistry* reported.

Dr. Rosenblad says the veterinary practitioners too often overlook the need for endodontic treatments. Such therapy is warranted probably more than most veterinarians and pet owners think, he says: "When I see a big dog come in, my first guess is, 'OK, which tooth is fractured?'"

Any dead tooth whose root is intact is a potential candidate. "Most teeth can be saved with root canals," Dr. LeVan says.

Put simply, a root canal involves removing the infected pulp tissue of dead tooth, then placing inert materials inside to make it a strong, usable, pain-free tool for eating and playing again.

Signs of Trouble
Vexingly, you may notice absolutely no change in behavior in your pet to alert you to trouble. A dog won't stop eating because he or she has a sore tooth, Dr. LeVan says.

"The biggest sign is no sign at all," Dr. Rosenblad says.

This can make it hard for an owner to notice a problem unless tooth brushings become routine. Dr. LeVan said she hears a common refrain from dog owners: "'It doesn't seem to be bothering him.'"

The dogs know, however. By the time they arrive at a veterinarian's office, their cases are often advanced. Usually the tooth is abscessed," Dr. LeVan says.

Signs may include excessive drooling, pawing or rubbing the face, teary eyes, greater tartar buildup on one side, sneezing, or a gray or purple discoloration of the tooth.

The Process, Step by Step

Usually a veterinary dentist performs the procedure, which is remarkably similar to a human root canal and requires many of the same supplies, Dr. LeVan says.

Any dog who can handle anesthesia is a good candidate, as long as a dental X-ray shows that a tooth lends itself to the procedure. With advances in anesthesia, a dog's age shouldn't keep a pet owner from pursuing treatment. "I've had dogs in their late teens," Dr. Rosenblad says.

First, a dog undergoes general anesthesia and local anesthesia. The veterinary dentist cleans out the dead tooth by using a series of files designed for dogs' teeth, then flushes the canal space and seals it with inert material to prevent bacteria from leaking back in.

Veterinary dentists can use a variety of sealing materials. Dr. LeVan uses a synthetic rubber that forms itself to the curves and the shape of the inside of the canal. When finished, she usually sends animals home with pain medication and sometimes antibiotics. Patients return for a follow-up visit to check their healing and return periodically for dental X-rays to make sure the tooth is fine. Complications are uncommon.

About Crowns

A worn tooth also requires a crown, which can be silver, gold or tooth-colored. Dr. LeVan's patients make two office visits. On the first visit, she removes a little tooth structure to prepare the tooth for the crown. On the second visit, she cements the crown onto the tooth. "A crown will help protect a tooth from re-fracture," Dr. LeVan says. "I recommend it for all teeth, but I really encourage it for major chewing teeth. I also recommend it for aggressive chewers and for police dogs."

Dr. LeVan favors a stainless-steel crown, which is the strongest and has proven itself over time, she says. Reinforcing that point, a study of forty-one metal full crown restorations in working dogs found that thirty-six crowns still were intact and functional when checked by researchers many months later, typically 30 months later, the *Journal of Veterinary Dentistry* reported. Five crowns

Metal crowns helped protect this bomb-sniffing dog's canine teeth. She had worn down the teeth so badly that they were in danger of fracturing and requiring root canal.

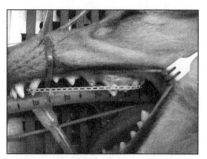

This dog's canine teeth pointed forward, and braces are being used to move them to their normal position.

were lost, usually because of subsequent injury and fracture of the tooth below the crown.

Tooth-colored porcelain crowns generally don't wear as well, and gold is too soft in dogs' mouths, Dr. LeVan says. Consider this: On average, a human's strongest bite is 500 pounds per square inch. Among dogs, it's 1,500 pounds per square inch. "They abuse their mouths much more than we do," Dr. LeVan says. "Anything that we would put in our hand, they put in their mouths."

Why Action Is Needed

Consider the canine tooth, the sharp, pointed tooth on either side of the upper and lower jaw. Dr. LeVan likens it to a human's thumb. "They use their mouths like a hand," she says. "So if they had a canine tooth extracted, it would be like losing a thumb. I really try to save those teeth."

She tries to protect any salvageable tooth but especially urges saving canine teeth and those used for tearing or shearing. Called the carnassial teeth, these shearers are the last premolars of the upper jaw and the first molars of the lower jaw. "Unfortunately, they're commonly fractured," Dr. LeVan says.

Dr. LeVan also has used a synthetic bone material called osteopromotive to fill in the bony defects around teeth to try to save them.

"If a dog loses a tooth as key as a lower canine, there is not much hard tissue support along the jawbone," she says.

Whatever the treatment decision, don't delay it, Dr. Rosenblad says: "The big, big picture statement is that any fractured tooth needs to be addressed."

Your Dog's Dental Future

Traditional surgical treatment of canine dental problems often required bulky metal materials that hindered a dog's ability to eat and prolonged periods with the animal under general anesthesia. Fortunately, new, less invasive dental tools and techniques are easing the pain and speeding the healing in dogs facing several dental problems.

"In the field of veterinary dentistry, there is literally a revolution occurring," says Peter Emily, a nationally renowned dentist who treats both people and animals. "We still have many unanswered questions, but we are definitely making progress at a rapid rate to improve the lives of dogs and cats."

Steven Holmstrom, a past president of the American Veterinary Dental Society who is in private practice in San Carlos, Calif., agrees: "We are able to do fewer extractions and save more teeth, thanks to new materials and techniques available in the past few years."

Advances include new bonding materials to better hold fillings in place; new tools that allow dentists to have better aim in solving problems and that eliminate burning the dog's mouth; and synthetic bone-grafting material that eliminates the need to transplant bone from another part of the body.

"In many cases, we can take in a dog with a sick, unhealthy mouth in the morning and send home a healthy dog by the end of the day," Dr. LeVan says. "You can truly make a major difference in a dog's life through dentistry." ■

18

Oh, Those Aching Footpads!

*Even tough, healthy pads can fall
victim to cuts, infections, and problems
related to the dog's diet.*

You can imagine what it feels like to walk on four aching paws if you've ever worn uncomfortable shoes on a long walk. The environment causes many canine footpad problems, and they're simple to treat. Other problems, medically based, require treatments that can be more complex.

Healthy pads are tough: thick enough to avoid tearing on sharp surfaces and rough enough to prevent slipping on smooth surfaces. Very active dogs have naturally tough feet from frequent exercise, but even the toughest pads can be sliced open by a piece of broken glass or jagged rock. Veterinarians often see cracked footpads caused by repeated exposure to chemicals such as rug shampoos, floor cleaners, garden preparations, and salt used to melt ice. Running on hot asphalt can also cause cracking. Some dogs lick their paws to ease the resulting soreness, worsening the situation. Hard, dry, crusty footpads—called hard pad disease—are a common sign of distemper.

"If all feet are affected, the most common cause is repeated exposure to some irritant, such as salt," says Gene Nesbitt, consulting dermatologist at Tufts Dermatology and Allergy Services. "It would be rare for a one-time exposure to an agent to cause cracking. If the agent is caustic, there is a higher probability of erosions, or sloughing, of some layers of the pad." The best treatment: remove the dog from the substance causing problems.

The most common problem associated with the feet that is secondary to allergies is inflammation between the pads and toes. Cracked pads can occur from chronic licking that results in a proliferation, or new cell growth, of the pad. Yeast infections can cause cracking, but the yeast is typically found between the toes rather than on the footpads. Veterinarians treat yeast infections, diagnosed by skin smears from the paw, with an antifungal.

Zinc and Pad Lesions

Zinc deficiency can also cause cracked footpads. "Pad lesions associated with zinc responsive dermatoses are from either Syndrome I, which is not a true deficiency but rather an absorption or utilization problem; or Syndrome II in growing puppies, which is caused by feeding a zinc deficient diet, diets high in phytates (a type of acid and source of phosphorus indigestible to carnivores) or calcium, or diets oversupplemented with minerals and vitamins," Dr. Nesbitt says.

"Lesions from Syndrome II are primarily hyperkeratosis, an excessive buildup of the top layer of the pad. Some cracks or fissures may result secondary to the hyperplasia," an abnormal increase in the number of normal new cells in tissue, he says. Hyperkeratosis is seen in both syndromes. Zinc slows down the maturation of the cells in the epidermis—the outer layer of the skin—resulting in slower sloughing of the dead cells. The dead cells then build up on the surface.

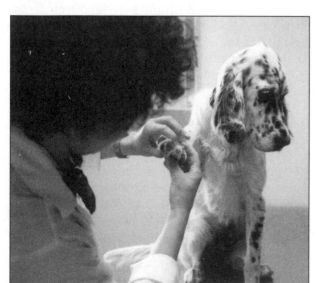

Depending on the diagnosis, veterinary dermatologists treat footpad problems with oral or intravenous zinc supplementation, corticosteriods, and adjustments to diet.

Alaskan Malamutes and Siberian Huskies are the two primary breeds affected by Syndrome I. Rapidly growing puppies or young adults of larger breeds, such as Great Danes, Dobermans, Beagles, German Shepherds, German Short-haired Pointers, Labrador Retrievers, Rhodesian Ridgebacks, and standard Poodles are also prone to it. Bull Terriers can suffer from a zinc deficiency resulting in acrodermatitis, an inflammation of skin in the paws or feet.

Veterinarians treat Syndrome I with zinc supplementation such as oral zinc sulfate, zinc gluconate, zinc methionine, or elemental zinc. They treat dogs who don't respond to oral medications with intravenous injections of zinc sulfate. Low-dose corticosteroids may help some dogs absorb the medicine from the intestinal tract.

Veterinarians treat Syndrome II by adjusting the diet. Hydrating the thickened pads is helpful. Soaking the pads in water and applying petroleum jelly or an ointment-based topical preparation help hold the moisture in the tissue.

Consider Booties

Dogs in winter climates sometimes develop footpad problems. Chunks of ice or snow attach to the hair between the pads. When the dog walks, the ice ball comes into contact with the surface and applies upward pressure into the bottom of the foot, causing pain and lameness. Small lacerations or localized inflammation may occur if the snow or ice isn't removed.

Booties are one solution to this problem. They also are an option for dogs who rough it on rocky trails, who have had paw or pad injuries, or who spend many hours walking over hot surfaces. (Dr. Nesbitt notes, however, that if the pads are eroded, it's generally recommended to allow exposure to air as much as possible.)

Most booties slide on like a sock and are held in place with Velcro. Those lined with polar fleece can be helpful for dogs who walk in rocky areas or on gravel and provide the best traction for snow.

Understand that your dog may not appreciate wearing booties. Some take to them immediately; others will lie on their backs and wave their booted paws in the air.

Some owners have had success letting their dogs wear booties around the house for short adjustment periods; others find the best strategy is to wait until just before a hike or run to put the booties on. Many dogs are too caught up in their exercise to stop and fuss with well-fitting booties.

Finally, a word of caution: be careful with sudden turns and stops: the enclosed claws and pads won't brake or react as sharply as they do when exposed.

Slipped Pads

Slipped pads develop when the thick top layer of pad skin peels off. Dogs routinely walked on soft surfaces or those who are always in a moist environment, either because their kennel gets wet or because they frequently in the water, generally have much softer pads with less protection against wear and rough surfaces.

"The pads normally become firmer with a more protective surface if they have routine exposure to hard surfaces," Dr. Nesbitt says. "If a dog has soft pads and is going to have repeated exposure to hard surfaces, there should be a gradual transition to give the pads time to toughen."

Treatment of slipped pads depends on the depth and severity of the problem. "If a secondary bacterial infection is present, which is fairly common, then systemic and/or topical antibiotics are indicated," Dr. Nesbitt says. "The dog should be prevented from licking the lesions by using an E-collar. The owner should prevent exposure to hard, irritating, or contaminated surfaces. If the lesions become soiled, wash them gently."

About Obsessive Licking

If your dog begins obsessively licking his or her paws, a visit to the veterinarian is in order. The dog may be suffering from a medical problem.

If the veterinarian provides a clean bill of health, it's possible the problem is behavioral, says Alice Moon-Fanelli, a Tufts assistant clinical professor and applied certified animal behaviorist. Paw licking can start as a

> *displacement behavior related to factors such as anxiety, stress or frustration, she says. If that's the case, "E-collars and foul sprays (aimed at deterring licking) generally are not helpful," Dr. Moon-Fanelli says. "You need to get to the root cause, be it medical or behavioral."*

Skin Diseases

Autoimmune diseases, notably the skin disease pemphigus, can cause problems such as pus-filled sores on the footpads. "Pemphigus is usually treated with high-dose corticosteroids and often concurrently with a chemotherapeutic agent such as asathioprine," Dr. Nesbitt says. "Some dogs with pemphigus foliaceus are either initially treated or maintained on tetracycline and niacinamide after the lesions are under control. Pemphigus vulgaris may be associated with sloughing of the pads."

Systemic lupus erythematosus, an inflammatory connective tissue disease, is associated with footpad ulcers and hyperkeratosis.

Footpads usually develop a more protective covering if owners routinely expose their dogs to hard surfaces (above).

German Short-haired Pointers are among the breeds prone to cracked footpads as a result of faulty zinc absorption or utilization (left).

Pododermatitis, an inflammation of the skin between the pads and toes, has several causes including foreign bodies such as fox-tails, local trauma, neoplasia, bacteria, contact irritants, clipper burns, allergies, fungus, demodicosis, Pelodera (a type of parasite), ticks, chiggers, hypothyroidism, autoimmune disease, drug reaction, zinc-responsive dermatitis, necrolytic migratory erythema (an erosive skin inflammation), and canine distemper.

"Lameness is variable depending on the location and severity of the lesions. Management is based on identification and treatment or prevention of the specific causes," Dr. Nesbitt says.

A skin disease called nasodigital hyperkeratosis tends to affect noses more than footpads of older dogs. If there is an underlying disease that is curable, then nasodigital hyperkeratosis may also be cured, but usually it's managed rather than cured. The majority of lesions must be controlled for a lifetime. In hyperkeratosis, keratin— the thick outer skin on the footpads—grows excessively. Ridges of excess keratin appear around pad edges.

Veterinarians diagnose it based on clinical signs and ruling out other causes. Then they trim the keratin. "At home, owners can hydrate the lesions by soaking the feet in water and applying wet compresses to the pads," Dr. Nesbitt says. "Then cover the lesions with a keratolytic agent, such as petroleum jelly, coal tar ointment, or tretinoin (Retinoid A) ointment. If the nose or pads are fissured, ointments containing antibiotics and corticosteroids are indicated."

When Injuries Occur

Sometimes, despite the best paw care, injuries do occur. A footpad injury can occur without an owner knowing why or when it happened. A dog may limp, and the owner then discovers a deep cut in the pad. Sometimes stitches are necessary. A surgeon is best able

Dogs who are frequently in water, like this miniature American Eskimo, can have soft footpads prone to injury.

to determine appropriate treatment.

Many pad injuries, even when pieces of the pad are missing, will usually heal by themselves. Applying antibiotic ointment can help prevent infection, and the pad will be back to normal within two weeks. If there is swelling or unusual heat in the pad, however, consult your veterinarian, in case an infection or abscess is brewing. And if your dog seems to have chronic foot pain, it could be a sign of a more serious medical condition. Your vet can help determine if any of these conditions are present.

"It is often difficult to get deep pad cuts to heal with suturing, even with debridement of the edges prior to suturing," Dr. Nesbitt says. "There is always a potential for a permanent fissure. The incidence of abrasion versus fissures is dependent upon the environment and the activity of the dog."

With or without surgery, the time for injuries to heal depends upon the cut's severity, depth, and the existence of a secondary infection.

Anatomy of the Foot

To understand how to take care of a dog's feet, you need to understand how they work. It may not be obvious at first glance, but your dog walks on his or her toes. If you imagine a dog's back leg as a human leg, you notice that a dog's "heel," called a hock, is only on the ground when a dog is sitting. On the front leg, the dog has a recognizable elbow leading to the wrist, which does not touch the ground when a dog moves. The dog rests not on the "palms," as a human on all fours would, but on the front toes.

Other animals, such as the horse, share this unusual anatomy, but the dog's pads and nails provide the paw with traction and shock absorption.

While all dogs' paws are anatomically similar, the huge variety of dog breeds means there are some key differences in the shape of the foot. Many working breeds have standards that call for compact or "cat feet." Breeds with "cat feet" include the Akita, Doberman Pinscher, Giant Schnauzer, Newfoundland, and Old English Sheepdog. Dogs with "hare feet" have two center toes that are longer than the side toes. Many toy breeds have

*hare feet, such as the Bedlington and Skye Terriers. Sight
hounds, such as the Borzoi and the Greyhound, also have
hare feet. Finally, some breeds that work in water are
bred for webbed feet. The Newfoundland, Chesapeake
Bay Retriever, Portuguese Water Dog, and German
Wire-haired Pointer all have webbing between their toes.*

Paw Grooming

Owners can do a lot to prevent injuries and protect their dogs' feet.
Be sure to include the paws in your regular grooming regimen. Keep
the fur trimmed between a dog's toes and pads so that ice balls don't
have a chance to collect when your dog is playing in the snow—or
nettles and burrs in the fields and woods. Make sure your dog's nails
are trimmed to the proper length—not quite touching the ground
when standing comfortably.

Always rinse your dog's paws with warm water after walking on
salty or sandy sidewalks. It's also a good idea to check your dog's
paws after hiking in the woods for burrs, twigs, or caked mud. After
rinsing off your dog's feet, towel them dry.

If the pads seem dry or brittle, try coating them with a little petroleum jelly or bag balm after going outside. Pad conditioners go
one step further by actually toughening the pads. They're not cheap,
but the products are worth it if they prevent injury especially if you
spend a lot of time outdoors with your dog. You should only use
these products if the pads are soft and injured. Otherwise, let nature take its course. Regular exercise is the best and healthiest way
to toughen your dog's pads. ■

19

Nailed!

*A little technique and good clippers can
make the process bearable for you and your dog.*

K eeping your dog's nails neatly trimmed is important for healthy feet. It is vitally important to teach your dog to accept nail trimming as part of his or her regular grooming routine. While dogs wear down their nails a bit on regular walks and other exercise, that simply isn't enough to keep nails as short as they should be—not quite touching the floor when the dog is standing.

If you start trimming nails for a puppy or a young dog, wait until he or she is resting quietly on the floor after a play session, gently clip off the tip end of one or two nails, feed the animal tasty treats and provide liberal praise. This dog will grow up thinking that nail trimming is a wonderful thing.

However, if the dog comes to you as an adult, he or she may have unpleasant memories associated with nail clipping. You may need to be very patient and use some of your best behavior modification skills—including praise and treats—to overcome resistance.

If the process is unbearable for you, your dog, or both of you after several efforts, remember that professional groomers can perform this task for you. Also, if your dog is undergoing sedation for teeth cleaning or any other procedure at the veterinarian, that is an excellent time to have the nails clipped.

Common Mistakes

There are several common mistakes that dog owners make when trimming nails. The first is clipping a nail too short (or "quicking" the dog) which causes pain and bleeding and immediately teaches the dog that nail trimming is not fun. Such an incident can require you to begin the desensitization process all over again.

If you clip the nail too much, use a styptic pencil to stop the bleeding. Or, if you don't have one handy, try baby powder or flour. Press the substance carefully against the wounded nail to cause clotting and stem the bleeding. Be aware that the bleeding may be profuse, and it is important that you stanch it as quickly as possible. Stay with the dog so that he or she does not lick the wounded nail and cause the bleeding to resume.

The second major mistake is trying to trim all the dog's nails in one session. This is fine once the dog learns that nail trimming is a positive thing, but until then, physically restraining a flailing, panicking animal while insisting that every nail is clipped only makes matters worse. Take the time to do nails one or two at a time, using treats and games to make it fun.

Finally, using poor equipment can make the even most accommodating dog fear nail trimming. Dull blades, tools with only poor visibility (this can result in quicking), and awkward clipper construction can turn nail trimming sessions into nightmares.

Above all, remember to steer clear of the quick—the nail's sensitive interior region that contains nerves and blood vessels—even though that means you will be clipping nails more frequently. In dogs with light-colored nails, the quick is visibly pink. But even if your dog's nails are dark, you can reduce the risk of painful (and bloody) quick-nicking.

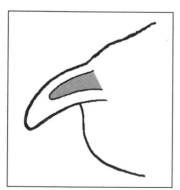

The goal of nail trimming is to clip enough extra nail to enable the dog to stand and walk comfortably, without clipping the nail so short that you hit the blood vessel. The pink vessel is easy to see in white nails; in black nails you have to clip conservatively, in small increments.

What to Do

Nail clipping really is really a safe and simple procedure, one that most owners can easily learn to perform on their dogs.

Remember, whether you handle the clipping or leave it to a professional, it's important that your dog's nails be trimmed regularly. Shelter workers and veterinarians tell horror stories of elderly dogs unable to walk because their nails have curled around and grown through their pads.

■ **Clip frequently.** Every time you clip your dog's nails, the quicks recede. Conversely, the quicks of infrequently trimmed nails grow outward.

■ **Settle for bits and pieces.** Clip off only narrow slices at a time. Stop when you see a black dot (the end of the quick) in the center of the gray-white cut surface.

■ **Use sharp trimmers.** Consider clippers equipped with guards to prevent you from cutting too close.

■ **Prevent squirming.** Teach your dog to be a more cooperative "clipee" by handling his or her feet often and using food treats as rewards during nail-trimming sessions. ■

Section III

Nutrition

20

Feeding a Balanced Diet

*Dog food occupies more shelf space than
baby food in many supermarkets; how do you know
whether you're feeding your dog "the right stuff"?*

Domesticated dogs depend on people to meet their nutritional requirements. As a dog owner who takes this responsibility seriously, you'll want to look closely at two things—your dog's nutritional needs and dog food labels.

A Balanced Diet

A complete, balanced diet provides your dog with energy and essential nutrients that the animal cannot manufacture on his or her own.

- **Protein** provides amino acids for tissue growth and repair. Protein should represent about 15 to 25 percent of an adult dog's food intake.
- **Fats** are your dog's primary energy source, providing essential fatty acids and transport for fat-soluble vitamins. An adult dog's diet should contain no less than 8 percent fat.
- **Carbohydrates**, while not essential, are another important energy source.
- **Vitamins** support enzyme function and help regulate nerve-impulse transmission and energy conversion.
- **Minerals** support nerve-impulse transmission, muscle metabolism, energy storage and transfer, and blood clotting, among other processes.

■ **Water**, the "forgotten nutrient," is essential for life. Your dog should always have access to clean, fresh water unless your veterinarian recommends otherwise.

> " ALTHOUGH A PARTICULAR FOOD MAY CONTAIN THE NECESSARY NUTRIENTS, THE NUTRIENTS ARE NOT AVAILABLE TO YOUR DOG IF THE FOOD DOES NOT TASTE GOOD AND IS NOT DIGESTIBLE. "

There is a delicate balance in the interactions between nutrients and a dog's cells and tissues. Attentive to that balance, reputable commercial dog-food manufacturers conduct continuous research and development and back the claims on their product labels (such as "nutritionally complete" or "complete and balanced") with actual feeding trials. Veterinarians emphasize the importance of checking to see if a particular manufacturer has noted "feeding trials" on its label to substantiate its nutritional claim

Although a particular food may contain the necessary nutrients, the nutrients are not available to your dog if the food does not taste good and is not digestible. (Ideally, your dog should be able to use 75 percent of the nutrients in his or her food.) Your dog's system absorbs more nutrients when food is highly digestible (not to mention palatable). Unfortunately, regulations don't require manufacturers to display digestibility percentages on their labels, but you can get that information (and other important statistics) from the manufacturer, many of whom have toll-free nutrition lines.

Avoiding Excess

According to Dr. Lisa Freeman, associate professor and veterinary nutritionist at the Tufts University School of Veterinary Medicine, "If you feed your dog a reputable brand of dog food that has been proven nutritionally complete through feeding trials, you don't need to supplement its diet with vitamins and minerals unless your veterinarian prescribes them to treat a deficiency or medical condition." In fact, harmful nutrient excesses from overfeeding or supplementing with vitamins and table scraps are far more common than nutrient deficiencies.

How much is enough? Consult the bag or can. Pet food manufacturers formulate their feeding guidelines based on what they believe is the correct equation for weight maintenance or growth.

How Much Is Enough?

Consider the following factors:

■ **Breed size**: *Small-breed dogs weighing less than 20 pounds need about 30 percent more calories, pound for pound, than dogs in the twenty- to seventy-five-pound range. Large-breed dogs over 75 pounds need about 15 percent fewer calories per pound of body weight than those in the twenty- to seventy-five-pound range.*

■ **Outside temperature**: *If your dog spends most of his or her time outside, the animal probably will probably need about 30 percent more calories in cold weather (approximately from December through February) than in the warmer months (June through August). A rule of thumb: with every 10 degree drop in temperature, dogs who spend significant time outdoors need about 7.5 percent more calories per day.*

■ **Metabolism**: *Dogs burn fat at different rates, just as humans do. Two dogs of similar size, age, and level of activity may need different amounts of food because of their metabolism. A nervous dog, a dog who moves in sudden bursts, and a "high-energy" dog will very likely burn calories at a higher rate than their more sluggish compatriots.*

■ **Neutering or spaying**: *A neutered or spayed dog can become more docile and less nervous, and as a result may require fewer calories.*

Wet or Dry?

Dog owners face several feeding quandaries. For example, should you feed your dog canned, soft-moist, or dry food? Dry food—the biggest seller—is nutrient dense, less expensive per unit of energy delivered, and convenient. Dry food doesn't spoil quickly, so it's suitable for free-choice (*ad libitum*) feeding. Also, its abrasive action can slow the buildup of tartar and plaque on your dog's teeth. However, some dogs find dry food unpalatable and therefore may not eat enough of it to meet their nutritional requirements.

Canned food has the longest shelf life, but because it spoils quickly once opened, it can't be left out for free-choice feeding. Many dogs, however, find it more palatable and digestible than dry food.

Keep in mind that if a diet has passed an Association of Animal Feed Control Officials feeding trial or nutrient profile standard, it contains what is believed to be an adequate level of nutrients.

Highly digestible soft-moist food, which often looks like ground hamburger, works well for free-choice feeding. But public concern about preservatives used in processing (and the food's higher relative cost) make it the least-popular commercial dog food.

The least common—and most problematic—feeding option is making your dog's food at home. Although you can concoct homemade dog food that is nutritionally balanced, most veterinarians advise against it. "People tend to create diets that might be good for them, but are not good for their dogs," observes Dr. Freeman.

If you are truly committed to the idea of making your dog's food yourself, design your recipe and monitor its performance with the help of a veterinary nutritionist.

Popular or Premium?

Another feeding dilemma is whether to buy popular or premium brands. People usually buy premium food from pet stores or pet-supply outlets, while popular (and "store label") brands are available at supermarkets. However, an increasing number of premium brands also are now available at supermarkets. Many popular brands use variable formulas—that is, the nutrient levels are consistent from batch to batch, but the ingredients vary. Premium brands are usually fixed-formula foods; you get consistent nutrient levels and consistent ingredients. If you're not sure which formula is used in your dog's food, call the manufacturer. Keep in mind that many dogs thrive on popular foods that have been proven, through feeding trials, to be nutritionally complete.

Cost may be a consideration for you. But remember that what really matters is the overall cost of feeding your dog, not how much an individual can or bag of food costs. Cup for cup, premium foods typically contain more calories and are more digestible than popular brands, so it takes less premium food to meet your dog's needs. Also, smaller amounts of highly digestible food mean smaller stools—another advantage of premium food.

Reading Between the Lines

Read past the bold claims that leap out from many dog-food labels and concentrate on the most important information: the statement of nutritional adequacy, the ingredient list, and the guaranteed analysis.

- *■ **Nutritional Adequacy Statement:** This tells you the food is nutritionally complete for "adult maintenance," "growth," or "all life stages." Most foods claim to meet nutritional levels established by the American Association of American Feed Control Officers (AAFCO), but before buying, make sure the manufacturer substantiates its claim with phrases like "feeding studies," "feeding tests," or "feeding trials" somewhere on the label. "A statement that verifies feeding trials were done should be a minimum requirement for the selection of an appropriate diet for your dog," says Dr. Freeman.*

- *■ **Ingredient List:** By law, ingredients must be listed by weight in decreasing order of predominance. But some companies choose to divide certain main ingredients into constituents to diminish their weight percentage (for example, "corn" becomes "corn gluten" and "flaked corn"). This practice may push ingredients perceived by consumers as "better" to the front of the list.*

- *■ **Guaranteed Analysis:** This list of minimum percentages of protein and fat and maximum percentages of fiber and moisture has a major shortcoming: it doesn't tell you the maximum amounts of protein and fat in* *the food—information you might need to help manage your dog's obesity, diabetes, kidney disease, or other condition. Note: The guaranteed analysis lists nutrient levels on an as-is basis, which won't help you compare one food to another. When comparing canned food (about 75 percent moisture) to dry food (about 10 percent moisture), you must compare dry-matter (that is, moisture removed) nutrient percentages. Your veterinarian or dog-food manufacturer can help you make this comparison.*

How Much?

The amount of food your dog needs depends on its size (although, per pound, large dogs need fewer calories than small dogs), individual metabolic rate, age, health status, and activity level. A typical dog's nutritional needs change several times over the course of his or her life-span—and even from season to season. (Requirements often decrease during the less-active winter months.)

In general, feed your dog the amount of nutritionally complete, highly digestible food necessary to maintain the animal's optimal body weight and good health. Adjust the amount recommended on the food label according to your dog's response.

Growing puppies, hard-working dogs, dogs living outdoors in cold weather, and lactating bitches have higher per-pound energy and nutrient requirements than the average adult dog. Dogs who sleep all day while their owners work need less fuel than a sled dog or a growing puppy. Older dogs tend to be less active than their younger counterparts and therefore require proportionally less energy. Talk to your veterinarian about the specific nutritional requirements for your dog.

When to Feed

Many of us decide when to feed our dogs based on convenience, but we should also consider other factors. For example, allowing your dog to eat free-choice—leaving food out all day for the animal to eat at will—is an invitation to obesity. And puppies and other dogs with high energy requirements need smaller, more frequent meals to give their digestive systems a chance to absorb the extra nutrients. A veterinarian may also recommend several small daily feedings to help manage the diet of a diabetic dog.

Most dogs will eat whatever you put in front of them (or whatever they can snitch), so arm yourself with knowledge and practice some discipline. Feeding your dog is the most basic form of health care you provide. Carefully read those dog food labels. Call the manufacturer, your veterinarian, or an animal nutritionist if you have any concerns or questions. And monitor your dog's response to any changes in diet by keeping tabs on his or her weight and general health through regular checkups.

Rib Test

*Is it time for your dog to lose (or gain) a few pounds?
To find out:*

■ *Stand behind your dog.*

■ *Place your hands over the sides of his or her chest
with your fingers spread over the rib cage.*

■ *Slide your hands gently over the ribs.*

*Can you readily feel the ribs? If you can't, your dog
is overweight. If the ribs protrude visibly, your dog is
too thin.*

No Fat Dogs

Obesity is technically defined as body weight 15 to 20 percent over a dog's optimal weight. And overfeeding is the most common cause. But before you assume that your feeding style is responsible, ask your veterinarian to check for potential medical causes.

Overweight puppies are at increased risk of developing diabetes mellitus and skin ailments. Obesity also exacerbates certain orthopedic, heart, and nervous-system diseases. Fat dogs are also higher-risk surgical patients, and they tend to have lower resistance to infection.

Although overfeeding dogs at any age can cause obesity, overfeeding during puppyhood can predispose a dog to lifelong obesity. While puppies are growing, both the number and size of their fat cells increase. Reducing the number of fat cells is much more difficult than shrinking their size.

Studies show that the incidence of obesity increases with age, and is more common in neutered dogs. It is an easier condition to prevent than treat. Treatment is straightforward but challenging—you have to make sure your dog's caloric intake is less than its energy expenditure. To slim down, an animal must take in less energy than is expended.

Given this fact, veterinary treatment for obesity usually focuses on controlled reduction of calorie intake and increased exercise compatible with an individual dog's health. To help your dog successfully lose weight, collaborate with your veterinarian, because frequently owners need to change their behavior.

If your dog's overall health permits, moderate exercise—such as brisk daily walks—is the best way to expend energy. "Most dogs out in the yard by themselves don't get much exercise," observes Dr. David Dzanis, a consultant and former veterinary nutritionist at the Food and Drug Administration's Center for Veterinary Medicine. That means owners have to make a point of scheduling in daily exercise for their dogs. Researchers also believe regular exercise may increase a dog's at-rest metabolic rate, boosting energy consumption even when the animal is napping.

For more on combatting obesity in dogs, see Chapter 24.

Treats and a Balanced Diet

Treats can be a double-edged sword. Cheese, kibble, bits of bread, and the like are powerful aids in training your dog with positive behavior modification techniques. Your dog comes—you give a treat. Your dog stops barking when commanded—you give a treat. Your dog offers paw or performs some other owner-favored behavior—you give a treat. But all those treats can add up to extra ounces and pounds.

If you choose to incorporate food as a reward into your training regimen, you may wish to consider some low- or no-calorie alternatives such as popcorn, ice cubs, rice cakes, raw vegetables (no onions), and fruit (no grapes).

And finally, remember—plenty of loving attention and praise is a healthy substitute for food treats. ■

21

Feeding Your Dog: Debunking the Myths

Caring owners match what they feed their dog to the animal's life stage, breed, activity level, size, and overall health.

Over the course of a lifetime, dogs change—and so do their nutritional needs. Their food intake must be balanced against where they are in their life cycle, along with numerous other factors. Frequently, however, desirous of giving their dogs "the best," some owners make erroneous—and potentially harmful—dietary assumptions.

Myth: More Is Better

If an adult-maintenance diet with 20 percent protein is good, then 35 percent protein must be better. Right? Not necessarily. While excess protein does no apparent harm to healthy dogs, too much protein may harm dogs with poorly functioning kidneys.

Healthy adult dogs require a minimum of 18 percent protein and 8 percent fat (on a "water removed" dry-matter basis) to maintain good health when at rest and free of stress. But hard-working dogs, canine athletes, or dogs who stay outdoors in cold weather may need greater quantities of certain nutrients—especially fat, which provides energy.

But when a dog's intake of calories (found most abundantly in fat, carbohydrates, and protein) consistently exceeds the calories expended, the dog becomes obese.

Your dog does not automatically need a diet change on his or her seventh birthday.

Myth: A Raw Diet Is Best

At first blush, a raw diet sounds logical; after all, isn't that the way dogs' ancestors ate in the wild for thousands of years? However, raw diets in general are not nutritionally balanced and actually can be dangerous to your dog's health due to harmful bacteria.

Myth: Pups Should Be Plump

Growing puppies do require more calories per unit of body weight and different concentrations of certain nutrients than adult dogs. You should therefore use puppy food with higher levels of protein and fat than in adult-maintenance food.

But don't go overboard. If puppies ingest too much energy-dense food, they may be headed for lifelong obesity. Both the size and number of fat cells increase in growing pups. Obesity caused by too many fat cells is difficult to combat because reducing the number of fat cells is much harder than reducing their size.

Moreover, too-rapid growth predisposes large-breed puppies (more than sixty-five pounds when mature) and giant-breed puppies (more than ninety pounds when mature) to skeletal problems such as hip dysplasia and osteochondrosis, both of which lead to arthritis).

Because high-potency puppy foods promote growth, experts suggest that owners of large- and giant-breed pups either feed less than the recommended amounts or use newly available growth formulas developed especially for large and giant breeds.

The new formulas promote slower, more gradual skeletal and muscular development because they are less calorie-dense and contain lower levels of calcium and phosphorus than traditional puppy foods.

Myth: Old Dogs Need "Senior" Diets

Some people think every dog over seven years of age needs a low-fat, low-protein "senior" diet rather than regular adult-maintenance food. But "older dogs are not a homogeneous group," cautions Dr. Lisa Freeman, associate professor and veterinary mutritionist at Tufts University School of Veterinary Medicine. "Treat your older dog as an individual and tailor its diet to its health, body condition, and activity level."

Veterinarians once also encouraged owners to feed older dogs low-protein diets to reduce the risk of kidney disease. But recent studies show that restricting protein below the adult-maintenance level is unnecessary for most healthy older dogs.

While slower metabolism and decreased activity can lead to weight gain in older dogs, some have a propensity to lose weight. To accommodate the varying needs of senior dogs, one dog-food manufacturer sells a senior diet for overweight elders and another formula for those who have trouble maintaining their weight as they age.

Remember, your dog is one of a kind and will not automatically require a special diet simply because he or she is young, old, or in between. Discuss diet with your veterinarian or a veterinary nutritionist. And when reading dog-food labels, be careful to distinguish between genuine nutritional information and marketing hype. ■

22

Feeding Newborn Puppies

*If you're a puppy's surrogate mother, you
will have an around-the-clock job for several weeks.
But look at the rewards.*

In an ideal world, all puppies would receive nurturing and sustenance from their moms (dams) during the first few critical weeks of their lives. Alas, some dams contract diseases and can't nurse, some reject their puppies, and some newborns lack the physical strength to nurse.

In such unfortunate cases, humans can help. But if you accept the role of surrogate dog mother, be prepared to stay busy around the clock for several weeks. There may also be heartbreak involved; some pups don't make it despite their human surrogate's conscientious efforts.

Early-puppyhood caretakers have two main jobs: providing a warm, draft-free environment (young pups can't regulate their body temperature and are vulnerable to chills) and feeding the pup the correct amount of appropriate nourishment at the right time.

Nothing Like Mom's Milk

In addition to essential nutrients, a dam's first milk (colostrum) contains antibodies that provide newborn pups with temporary immunity against disease. If at all possible, puppies should ingest colostrum during the first few hours after birth. If the mother or another nursing "foster dog" is not available, you'll have to hand-feed the puppy—and do your best to isolate the animal from

Puppies who can nurse from their mother in their early days stay the best chance of a healthy life.

sources of infection to compensate for the lack of maternally provided immunity.

To make sure hand-fed pups receive proper nutrition, most veterinarians recommend commercial milk-replacement formulas, available as ready-to-feed liquids or mixable powders. "Homemade formulas are less convenient, and not all recipes provide adequate nutrition for a newborn puppy," notes Dr. Lisa Freeman, associate professor and nutritionist at Tufts University School of Veterinary Medicine. Cow's milk alone is definitely inadequate because it lacks sufficient calories, protein, calcium, and phosphorus. Whether you use a commercial or homemade formula, keep it refrigerated to prevent growth of harmful bacteria and warm each serving to about 100 degrees Fahrenheit just before feeding time.

Tube or Bottle?

You can get formula into a pup through either a nipple bottle or feeding tube. Bottle feeding takes longer and increases the risk that the puppy will accidentally inhale formula into his or her lungs. Tube feeding, which involves delivering formula through a feeding catheter passed into the puppy's stomach, is generally safer and faster—and the most practical method for a newborn who lacks a sucking reflex. Both techniques require some expertise, so ask your veterinarian or an experienced puppy raiser for a demonstration. With either method, it's important to wash all feeding utensils in hot, soapy water after each use.

Weight Watching

When using commercial preparations, follow the mixing instructions and weight-based feeding guidelines on the label, remembering that you may need to increase or decrease listed amounts to suit individual pups. "For the first couple of days, it's better to err on the side of underfeeding," says Dr. Freeman, who explains that overfeeding (or feeding a formula that's too concentrated) can result in diarrhea. Young pups dehydrate rapidly, so if diarrhea persists for more than twenty-four hours, have your veterinarian check out the pup. During a pup's first week, feeding will be required every two hours. Subsequently, feed the total daily amount over six equally sized and spaced-apart feedings.

Steady weight gain is the best measure of whether a hand-fed pup is receiving appropriate nourishment. In general, a pup should gain one to two grams of weight daily for each pound of the animal's expected adult weight. For example, a dog you anticipate will weigh 50 pounds as an adult should gain 50 grams (1.75 ounces) to 100 grams (3.5 ounces) per day. Keep accurate records of how much formula the pup consumes at each feeding and how much weight is gained each day.

Challenges and Rewards

Until your puppy is about three weeks old, he or she will need help urinating and defecating. To stimulate these important bodily functions, gently massage your pup's anal and genital area after feeding with a cotton ball dipped in warm water.

If you embark on the demanding task of hand-rearing a puppy, it could be the most rewarding canine caretaking experience you ever have. The bonding experience is unique, and it's quite possible you will have saved the puppy's life. But before you take on this responsibility, honestly ask yourself if you have enough time and energy. If not, your veterinarian or local humane society may be able to find a suitable surrogate. ■

23

Food Allergies

*While food allergies cannot be cured,
with proper diagnosis and treatment,
they can be managed.*

Food allergies affect 5 to 10 percent of dogs. And those allergies may develop years after a dog has been eating the same foods. An allergy is a type of immune-system response to a substance the body perceives as "foreign." Because the allergic response builds up over time, a pet may not show symptoms for a long time. When a dog "suddenly" develops a food allergy, he or she is actually just manifesting symptoms of a condition that has been developing for some time.

Unlike humans, who tend to respond to allergens with sneezing and runny eyes, dogs with allergies tend to exhibit skin problems. Most commonly, the dog's skin becomes inflamed and itchy around the feet, face, ears, armpits, and groin. Dogs who rub their faces on the carpet, as well as dogs who have chronic ear infections, may be showing signs of allergy. Some dogs also have gastrointestinal symptoms, such as vomiting and diarrhea.

Making a diagnosis that a dog has a food allergy is not a simple matter. Dogs are more commonly allergic to flea bites than to food, and many dogs have seasonal allergies to pollen or to other inhalants. Itchy skin is also a common sign of other conditions such as sarcoptic mange.

Dietary Changes

Like humans, most dogs who develop allergies are sensitive to a protein in their diet, such as beef, chicken, or dairy products. Because of this, lamb and rice formulas were originally introduced as "hypoallergenic" diets. However, some dogs are allergic to lamb, a reaction veterinarians are seeing more frequently now that lamb-based dog food is widely available. Dogs can also be allergic to proteins in other ingredients, such as corn, soy, or wheat.

Although many pet owners are suspicious of additives like preservatives or coloring, very few dogs are allergic to them. "Allergies to additives are extremely rare," says Dr. Gene Nesbitt, a veterinary dermatologist who is a clinical professor at Tufts University School of Medicine. "Preservatives are almost never identified as the cause of a food allergy. People think they are, but there's no scientific basis for that belief."

When a food allergy is suspected, some owners are able to make a quick fix by switching foods. However, some dogs are allergic to more than one ingredient in their food. To discover which ingredient is the culprit in a dog's diet, most veterinarians recommend an elimination diet. The creation of an elimination diet is made individually, based on each dog's food history. Owners must know what sources of protein and carbohydrate to which their dogs have been exposed, and they must pick totally new foods to test on their animals. Your veterinarian may be able to recommend a product for your dog. Some owners opt to cook for their dog during the trial period. Further, keep in mind that allergies to food coloring or other additives can be hard to pinpoint.

The special diet should be fed for a period up to ten weeks. Most food-allergic dogs will show improvement by then, although a few breeds, such as Labrador retrievers and cocker spaniels, seem to

Like humans, most dogs who develop allergies are sensitive to a protein in their diet.

need longer trials. During that time, only the elimination diet food and water should be consumed—no table scraps, chewies, or biscuits are allowed. Even chewable medications can be a problem. Ask your veterinarian for a capsule or pill form of the dog's drugs.

Most veterinarians like to check on the dog's progress during the elimination diet. If symptoms abate and the dog's condition improves, you can assume that something in your dog's original food caused the condition. However, if you want further proof, you can switch your dog back to his or her original food. Most signs of food allergy will reappear in a week or two.

If the test is successful, many owners simply keep their dogs on the elimination diet they have been using. Some of these specialty diets can be expensive, however, and owners may wish to cautiously introduce different foods to pinpoint the specific ingredient to which their dog is allergic. This is a time-consuming process, as each new food needs to be introduced into the dog's diet over a period of two weeks so that owners may observe any changes in the dog's condition.

Sometimes an elimination test is unsuccessful. Owners need to be certain in this case that their dogs have not been eating any other food or substances during the test. At times, veterinarians will ask owners to keep their dogs on a diet for a longer period of time. Further tests may be required, such as a skin biopsy, and a referral to a veterinary dermatologist may also be recommended.

New Approach: Downsized Proteins

A new trend in the field of canine food allergy focuses on the size of the protein in food—not on the plant or animal source. It may lead veterinarians to diagnose and manage food allergies more quickly and simply. Scientists believe that small proteins are less allergy-provoking than big proteins. "If you chemically cut proteins into smaller molecular chunks, the immune system is less likely to recognize them as foreign substances," explains Steven S. Hannah, Ph.D., a nutrition scientist at Ralston Purina Co. in St. Louis, whose company markets therapeutic canine diets made from small, low-molecular-weight proteins.

Theoretically, with the "small protein" approach, you don't have to worry about finding novel ingredients. Manufacturers claim that such diets can help veterinarians reliably diagnose food allergies in four to six weeks. They also claim that you can feed these diets over the long term to manage food allergies—with little or no risk of subsequent allergic reactions.

The Jury Is Still Out

But before discussing these new therapeutic diets with your veterinarian, remember that many dogs are successfully diagnosed and treated for food allergies using the time-tested elimination-diet technique. Moreover, therapeutic diets don't undergo the rigorous pre-market efficacy testing the U.S. Food and Drug Administration requires of veterinary pharmaceuticals before they are allowed on the market. Caution is also advisable because scientists have only demonstrated the efficacy of low-molecular-weight proteins in the laboratory.

"There is often a difference between what goes on in a test tube and what goes on in a dog," notes Dr. Lisa Freeman, associate clinical professor and veterinary nutritionist at Tufts University School of Veterinary Medicine.

Your veterinarian will also want to carefully examine the labels of these new diets. He or she will probably pay special attention to the protein content of all the ingredients—not just the major protein source—and check the nutritional adequacy statement. Some therapeutic diets are labeled "intended for intermittent feeding only," meaning they may not be nutritionally adequate for long-term use.

Food allergies can't be cured, but they can be managed successfully by careful feeding. Dogs who are allergic may also develop allergies to their new food, so owners should be prepared for this possibility. In any event, dogs with signs of food allergies should always be evaluated by a veterinarian. ■

24

Weighty Matters

Like people, dogs can put on weight so gradually the extra pounds can go unnoticed. But those stealth pounds can endanger your dog's health.

O besity is the most common nutritional disorder in dogs. By some estimates, at least a quarter of all dogs weigh more than 20 percent more than their optimal weight, which is a common definition of obesity. Although a large proportion of these canines are senior citizens, youngsters are by no means immune to packing on the pounds.

Just as in humans, canine obesity contributes to various physical ailments: obese dogs have a greater incidence of skin disease (dermatosis) than do their svelte counterparts, and have a higher incidence of endocrine disorders such as diabetes mellitus, a malfunction of the body's glucose-uptake system. And since fat cells need oxygen too, a fat dog's heart and lungs work harder, exacerbating any existing heart and respiratory conditions. Excess pounds also put extra stress on skeletal joints, aggravating musculoskeletal disease. Furthermore, obese male dogs tend to produce fewer healthy sperm, and pregnant obese dogs have an increased risk of complications during labor (dystocia).

Recognizing Obesity

Owners often don't notice their pet's subtle weight gain and don't realize their dog is overweight until a veterinarian, groomer, or trainer points out the extra pounds. Regularly assess your dog's weight to determine whether your animal needs an adjustment in his or her feeding and exercise routine. Keeping your dog slim is a lot easier than working to lose weight once the excess pounds have piled up.

You can keep track of your dog's weight by periodically weighing it at a nearby veterinary clinic. You can also assess your animal's body condition with the "rib test." When you stroke your dog's sides, you should be able to easily feel—but not see—the animal's ribs. And when you look at your pet's silhouette from above, you should be able to see an obvious waistline. If you have difficulty feeling the ribs or seeing the waistline, your dog is overweight. And if you can't feel the ribs at all or see any waistline, your dog is extremely overweight.

> 66 REGULARLY ASSESS YOUR
> DOG'S WEIGHT TO DETERMINE WHETHER
> YOUR ANIMAL NEEDS AN ADJUSTMENT
> IN HIS OR HER FEEDING AND
> EXERCISE ROUTINE. 99

Fatness Factors

Obesity doesn't happen overnight. Typically, an overweight dog has been consuming more calories than he or she is expending for months or years. The cause of this imbalanced state of affairs is usually a combination of insufficient energy expenditure—due to lack of physical exercise—and excessive energy consumption—due to eating too much tasty, energy-dense dog food and too many treats.

In addition, a dog's resting metabolic rate (RMR), which determines how many calories the animal expends to maintain normal body functions, may decrease after neutering or spaying. Owners can easily prevent their animals from becoming rotund after spaying or neutering by decreasing their food consumption and keeping them physically active.

Slimming Down

If your dog is overweight, your veterinarian can help you determine how many pounds the animal needs to lose. And if the dog shows other signs of illness, the clinician may want to check for a medical disorder such as hypothyroidism (insufficient thyroid-hormone production) that could contribute to obesity. You and your veterinarian can work together to develop a weight-loss program that will help your dog gradually shed those extra pounds.

Most successful weight-loss programs employ a three-pronged approach: decreasing calories, changing the dog's and owner's food-related behavior, and increasing exercise.

■ **Calorie Reduction**: "You definitely need to cut down the number of calories your dog eats, which often means meal feeding as opposed to free-choice feeding," says Dr. Lisa Freeman, associate clinical professor and veterinary nutritionist at Tufts University School of Veterinary Medicine. Meal feeding (controlled feeding) is a good idea even if you switch from a regular dog food to a reduced-calorie dog food because even with a "lite" diet, your dog runs the risk of consuming the same number of calories or even more by eating larger quantities. You should also be aware that not all low-calorie foods are created equal. Make sure your dog's "low-cal" food actually contains fewer calories than the food the animal had been eating.

■ **Behavior Modification**: We all enjoy praising our dogs, which often includes food treats. But many of our dogs have become consummate beggars, managing to look ravenous while we prepare and eat our meals. As a result, keeping track of and controlling the amount of calories your dog consumes can be difficult. We recommend you keep begging dogs out of the kitchen during meal preparation and meals. And instead of giving a food treat, give your dog attention and affection.

■ **Increased Exercise**: Regular exercise increases the amount of energy your dog expends. Begin with low-intensity exercise for short periods of time. Taking your dog for several short walks each day is a good way to begin. Gradually increase the length of your walks and include more intense exercise such as jogging or an energetic game of fetch. If your dog has arthritis or other health problems, talk to your veterinarian about how much exercise is safe for your pet.

If your dog becomes "nudgy" while dieting, try feeding it a low-calorie, high-fiber food. "Some animals may drive their owners less crazy if they are on a high-fiber diet," says Dr. Freeman. You might also try feeding your dog small amounts of raw carrots; green beans;

or unbuttered, air-popped popcorn to satisfy the animal's hunger without adding too many calories. And offering more frequent meals (but the same total quantity per day) will help satisfy some dieting canines. Most of all, when your dog looks you in the eye with that pitiful gaze, remind yourself that the diet is in his or her long-term best interest and stick to your guns.

Nutrient Deficiencies

Most owners worry more about nutritional deficiency than they do about obesity. But this concern is misplaced since obesity is extremely common, while nutritional deficiencies are extremely rare. "As long as you feed a good-quality commercial diet made by a reputable manufacturer and tested through feeding trials, you are very unlikely to see any deficiencies," says Dr. Freeman.

Most commercial foods contain enough vitamins and minerals to meet the needs of the vast majority of dogs. And many manufacturers add extra nutrients to compensate for any possible nutrient loss during storage.

Ironically, owners who are trying to avoid nutritional deficiencies by supplementing with vitamins and minerals may actually cause deficiencies. Too much of one type of vitamin or mineral may interfere with the absorption of another. If your dog or puppy is one of those rare canines with a specific need for an additional nutrient, your veterinarian can advise you on an appropriate supplement.

A dog can also suffer from a nutritional deficiency if the owner provides a good quality commercial food but then adds "people food" such as hamburger. The added topping dilutes and unbalances the nutrients in the commercial diet, which can lead to a nutritional deficiency. Poor-quality commercial food can also cause nutritional deficiency, as can homemade diets. While owners can make their own nutritionally balanced dog food, doing so requires following a carefully formulated scientific recipe that meets a dog's complex nutritional needs. ■

25

Preservatives

*Contrary to some beliefs, preservatives maintain
dog food's safety and nutritional integrity and pose
little danger to your animal's health.*

Tocopherols. Ethoxyquin. Butylated hydroxyanisole and hydroxytoluene. They sound like contents of a chemist's shelves. In fact, they're synthetic preservatives that make your dog's food safe.

Even so, with such strange names, it's little wonder that rumors abound about preservatives. They're perhaps the most misunderstood, most maligned pet food ingredient. At one time or another, they've been rumored to cause cancer, autoimmune diseases, stillborn pups, difficult pregnancies, and liver and kidney disease. A scare about preservatives such as ethoxyquin left both pet owners and pet food manufacturers scrambling to find alternatives.

Are preservatives really that bad? Are they dangerous? What alternatives do you have to feed your dog?

"Preservatives are used primarily to maintain safety and nutritional integrity," says Rebecca Remillard, a veterinary nutritionist at Angell Animal Medical Center in Boston, Massachusetts, who is board-certified by the American College of Veterinary Nutritionists. "There is a small amount of bacteria and other bugs in all foodstuffs. If you have some fresh food on the counter for twenty-four hours, those bacteria are going to grow, and the food is going to go bad. If you look at the [U.S. Department of Agriculture's] guidelines for thawing meat, it gives you an idea how perishable food is. Bugs multiply quickly in warm temperatures and moisture, and when significant numbers of them are ingested, they will make you and your pet sick."

> 66 THE TRUTH IS THAT WITHOUT
> PRESERVATIVES, YOU'D HAVE MANY MORE
> PROBLEMS WITH DOG FOOD THAN YOU
> DO WITH PRESERVATIVES. 99

The truth is that without preservatives, you'd have many more problems with dog food than you do with preservatives. Fat—a vital ingredient in all pet food—spoils quickly without a preservative, and your dog can become very sick eating rancid dog food.

"There's some evidence indicating eating rancid food can cause cell abnormalities that can lead to cancer, which is precisely what people who are afraid of preservatives are concerned about," Dr. Remillard says. "By preventing rancidity, preservatives actually may be preventing cancer."

Preservatives, as the word implies, keep food fresh by preventing oxidation or the breakdown of molecules within it. They're essential in all dry pet foods and those not processed through canning or freezing. Even then, preservatives don't last forever, and common ones break down over time.

First, to clear up some common misconceptions: Most preservatives are synthetics, even the so-called natural ones such as vitamin A and E (tocopherols) and ascorbic acid, or vitamin C. These preservatives are often used in "natural" pet food, although the sources may be derived chemically.

They're vitamins, Dr. Remillard says, "but they've been chemically altered to function as preservatives and make them biologically unavailable to the pet. For example, a tocopherol used as a preservative is not the same as the vitamin E that your body can use. These vitamins have been chemically altered but originated from natural antioxidants."

Many pet food manufacturers, aware of some consumers' desire to feed a more natural food, use these so-called natural preservatives. The problem: There's no true definition of what's considered natural, according to the U.S. Food and Drug Administration. "Natural" is a nice marketing label, but you may not get what you consider natural.

Two Owners, Two Opinions
On Safe Dog Food

Steve Dale of Chicago, Ill., author and host of Animal Planet Radio, feeds a mix of commercial foods to his dogs, Chaser, a Brittany, and Lucy, a North American Shepherd. "I'm concerned about preservatives for both myself and my pets, but preservatives are prevalent in our foods," he says.

Even vegetarians and vegans would be hard-pressed to find foods without preservatives.

"I'm more concerned about a balanced diet for my pets and the safety of the food," Dale says. "I know that I'm not going to worry about salmonella and other nasty bacteria when I open a bag of dog food. What's more, I trust a lot of the research the pet food companies do because I believe they care about pets. They're not likely to include something bad for your pet. Even from an economic standpoint, it makes sense for them to want your pets to be around a long time."

Liz Palika of Oceanside, Calif., author of The KISS Guide to Raising a Puppy *(DK Publishing), feeds her two Australian Shepherds, Riker and Dax, dog food preserved through dehydration. "There are too many unanswered questions regarding the safety of preservatives when fed long-term and too many conflicting answers," Palika says.*

"One group says ethoxyquin is perfectly safe, for example, while another group screams that it is deadly. I have done enough research to be concerned about the various preservatives used in most foods," she says. "Therefore, until I get a consensus, or my questions are answered to my own satisfaction, I will avoid them as much as possible."

Short Shelf Life

Many of the so-called natural preservatives don't have the shelf life of other chemical preservatives, so it's important to choose a dog food that's as fresh as possible. Most dog food companies have freshness dates or codes to identify when the food was manufactured. Contact the company—a toll-free number usually is provided on the bag—to find out how to read the codes if they're unclear to you.

Generally, you don't want a bag older than six months, and the fresher the better. An opened bag shouldn't smell spoiled or rancid. If the food inside looks gray or stinks, throw it out or return it to the store for a refund.

"The bigger pet food companies have taken control not only of the manufacture but also the shipping and storage of their foods to be sure that what you receive is fresh and in excellent condition," Dr. Remillard says. "Some pet food manufacturers feed a portion of their food product to dogs or cats at their own facilities as part of routine quality control procedures. If these animals do not eat the food as expected, they hold the shipment for additional testing. They may not ship the food at all because it is more cost effective to scrap a batch before it leaves the plant than to have to track it down later and take the bad publicity."

Preservatives and Canned Food

As long as manufacturers process food, they'll add preservatives to protect it from being spoiled. As a result, it's no surprise canned food also contains preservatives, but at lower levels because canning itself preserves food.

Depending on where the manufacturer obtained it, the fat in dog food will already contain a preservative to prevent it from becoming rancid. "Almost all fat sources shipped in the [United States] are preserved," Dr. Remillard says. "If you want to feed fewer preservatives, canned food is an option."

During canning, certain colors fade in dog food. The manufacturer may use sodium nitrite or another preservative to keep it looking fresh. "These are the same preservatives in human foods," says Dr. Robin Downing, owner of Windsor Veterinary Clinic in Windsor, Colorado, and an affiliate faculty member at Colorado State University College of Veterinary Medicine and Biomedical Sciences.

"The most common is mixed tocopherols, or vitamin E. Even so [manufacturers] use a miniscule amount. We're talking parts per million here, not milligrams," says Dr. Downing, author of *Pets Living With Cancer: A Pet Owner's Resource* (American Animal Hospital Association).

Preservatives and Allergies

Preservatives are the most expensive ingredient in dog food, so it behooves the manufacturer to use as little as possible, Dr. Remillard says. Pets who show sensitivity to ingredients in pet food are more likely to show it to the protein or grain source rather than preservatives. What's more, she says, no single documented case has been reported of a pet with allergies to a particular preservative. "They're more likely to have food intolerance to major ingredients like chicken or corn than a micro ingredient. The owner should look at those major ingredients first."

While they may stir controversy, preservatives are here to stay in pet food. The benefits far outweigh the perceived risks by preventing spoilage, dangerous bacteria and loss of nutrients. They keep food fresh and edible, so your dog can reap the optimal nutrition in his or her diet.

Ethoxyquin: 'The Most Effective At Lowest Dose'

Ethoxyquin is one of the preservatives some dog owners and holistic veterinarians have targeted as a health risk. It was used for more than thirty years without problems until the early 1990s, when pet owners reported allergies, liver disease, organ failure, skin disorders, cancer, and reproductive problems to the U.S. Food and Drug Administration's Center for Veterinary Medicine. The problem: no substantiated evidence exists that ethoxyquin or any other ingredient in the pet food was or is to blame.

"The so-called problems with ethoxyquin were debunked a long time ago," says Dr. Downing. "It's a very safe and effective preservative. It does occur naturally, but in order for it to be cost effective, manufacturers produce it."

Still, owners were concerned and scrambled to find food without the ingredient. Manufacturers, sensitive to the market, changed to tocopherols, BHA or other preservatives to keep customers, not because they considered ethoxyquin was harmful.

Recent studies by Monsanto, ethoxyquin's manufacturer, showed that feeding ethoxyquin causes an increase in liver-related enzymes in the bloodstream and an accumulation of a hemoglobin-related pigment in the liver. Its effect on animals' long-term health is not known.

However, the Center for Veterinary Medicine asked pet food manufacturers to voluntarily lower their maximum use of ethoxyquin to 75 parts per million.

Should you be worried if you're feeding a food containing ethoxyquin?

"There's no proof that ethoxyquin causes anything," says Dr. Remillard. "It is the most effective preservative at the lowest dose. The Monsanto studies were done with multiple high dose levels of ethoxyquin in a multi-generational study."

This means the dogs were fed high doses and bred. Their puppies ate high doses, grew to adulthood and bred for several more generations so that ethoxyquin could accumulate in the dogs if problems were to occur. It took several generations before there was any change in tissue.

The message for dog owners is clear: ethoxyquin is unlikely to cause serious health problems.

Despite the very low level of risk, if you are concerned about ethoxyquin's potential effects, switch to a brand using tocopherols or other preservatives. ■

26

Should You Supplement?

*The experts say there's no
need to supplement your dog's
diet unless he or she is ill.*

M any owners, worried their dogs aren't getting the right nutrition, have turned to supplements. They're chopping raw food or poaching chicken with rice. They're adding calcium, vitamins, and nutraceuticals such as glucosamine and shark cartilage to the daily diet, hoping to ward off arthritis.

Their efforts may be well intentioned, but supplementation has stirred considerable controversy. Among the reasons: balancing vitamins and minerals can be tricky, with potentially harmful results if not done correctly. And, the government doesn't regulate neutraceuticals, defined in *Webster's Third New International Dictionary, Unabridged*, as "a foodstuff ... that is held to provide health or medical benefits ... in addition to its basic nutritional value."

Further, some supplements once considered safe—such as L-tryptophan, kava kava and ephedrine—have been linked to serious health problems in people.

Do Supplements Help?

Ultimately, the question is whether supplementing their diet helps our dogs. The answer from veterinary nutritionist Rebecca Remillard is a resounding no. It's simply unnecessary except in cases of illness and disease, and then only upon the advice of a veterinarian.

"Healthy dogs don't need supplementation if they're fed a complete and balanced commercial dog food," Dr. Remillard says. "If you believe the dog food is complete and balanced, then why supplement?"

Furthermore, most owners use veterinary supplements that have very low dosages, she says. "They don't understand that the dog food doesn't need these supplements, and in most cases the amounts are so low they have a negligible effect."

Neutraceuticals have become popular in recent years, but they do not carry the U.S. Food and Drug Administration's blessing. These substances are considered "unapproved food additives," Dr. Remillard says. This means anyone can manufacture them, and there's no oversight to determine if the active ingredients are actually present.

> " MANY OF THE MEDICINAL EFFECTS OF HERBAL SUPPLEMENTS, WHICH CAN HAVE AN UNREGULATED AMOUNT OF A SUBSTANCE, ARE AT BEST ANECDOTAL. "

What's in these products is anyone's guess, she says. "No one is watching out for the consumer. There's no quality control and no guarantee that it's safe or efficacious. Even in human supplements, you'll find very few USP seals [approval from the United States Pharmacopeia, a standards-setting organization] on the label."

Arthritis supplements, such as glucosamines and chondroitins, are a different matter. "They are not nutritional supplements but pharmacological agents, " Dr. Remillard says. "They're closer to a drug than to a nutritional supplement. There is some indication that these work in people, but there is no clear evidence that they work in animals yet."

Many of the medicinal effects of herbal supplements, which can have an unregulated amount of a substance, are at best anecdotal. Owners could spend a lot of money and see little if any advantage. "You're transferring money from your wallet to someone else's with very little documented benefit to the dog," Dr. Remillard says.

She does offer a caveat about choosing a commercial dog food: "It must be formulated to AAFCO guidelines." AAFCO—the Association of Animal Feed Control Officials—is made up of government regulators and pet food industries experts who establish guidelines for nutrition. For a dog food to be "complete and balanced," the manufacturer must prove it meets or exceeds AAFCO guidelines through feeding trials or formulation testing.

Excessive Amounts Can Do Harm

Here are some of the positive and negative effects of some popular supplements. It can't be repeated too often: check with your dog's veterinarian before supplementing the animal's diet.

■ *Calcium: Excessive amounts can cause bone deformities and interfere with absorption of other minerals. Too little can cause bone loss.*

■ *Vitamin C: Too much can cause diarrhea. There is no AAFCO daily requirement for dogs because they manufacture more than adequate amounts of Vitamin C.*

■ *Glucosamine: No apparent requirement. Can interfere with diabetes because it's a carbohydrate source.*

■ *Omega-3 fatty acids: No apparent requirement.*

■ *Zinc: Excessive amounts may be toxic and interfere with absorption of other minerals. Too little can cause hair, skin, immunity and reproductive disorders.*

■ *Meat: An All-meat diet can cause a phosphorus/calcium imbalance. Raw meat may contain harmful bacteria that can be transferred to humans.*

■ *Probiotics: Digestive bacteria or "good bacteria" that live in the intestines. It's possible that stomach acid destroys the bacteria before they reach the intestines.*

Digestibility Is Key

Robin Downing, a veterinarian and affiliate faculty member of Colorado State University College of Veterinary Medicine and Biomedical Sciences, advocates feeding premium dog food. "There's a reason why generic foods only cost five or ten bucks for a fifty-pound bag. You're getting what you pay for. When you look at dog food, you should be concerned about digestibility."

Digestibility, the amount of food not appearing in the feces, is an indication of the nutrition the dog can actually use. Most regular, commercial dog foods have reasonable digestibility—better than 80 percent—meaning that, while they meet AAFCO guidelines, the percentage of usable nutrients is lower per cup than a highly digestible (90 percent) food. Therefore, a pet owner must feed more of the less digestible food to obtain the same nutrition as a highly digestible dog food.

Higher digestibility numbers mean you'll have to feed less food and clean up the yard less often, but the cost per day may very well be the same. And some amount of fiber and stool residue is necessary for a healthy bowel. Foods with low digestibility use added dietary fibers, which remain undigested and eliminated. While many dog food companies don't print digestibility numbers on their bags, you can call manufacturers or visit their Web sites to get the figure for a particular dog food. Moderate to high fiber diets are beneficial for some dogs.

Dr. Remillard, on the other hand, finds "premium" food a very large gray area. "You can no longer tell whether the dog food is a 'premium' dog food by the company, the price, or even where you buy it. There are companies that will make the same dog food and market it under different brands and prices. There are no nutritional rules as to what is 'premium' food. 'Premium' is a marketing term, and anyone can place that term on their product, for it has no legally binding definition," she says. "What you must do is read the label, and if the food has passed an appropriate AAFCO feeding protocol, you can try that food on your dog to see if it works for him."

What is 'Complete'?

Despite AAFCO guidelines, some owners believe that regular or premium bags or cans of dog food must be nutritionally incomplete.

"Some people don't trust pet food companies for whatever reason, but we have a reputation to maintain," says Dan Carey, a veterinarian who works in research and development for pet food manufacturer Iams Company. "We're going to say things that we know are true, and we're not going to do something that could cause a backlash."

However, folklore perpetuated through pet owners and on the Internet suggests that pets require more than AAFCO guidelines. With so much conflicting information, it's tempting for owners to toss supplements at their dogs in the hopes of fixing a perceived problem.

In fact, the AAFCO guidelines labeled as "minimum" are not the minimum amounts required by the dog. They are the minimum amounts required to be in the food. Few owners truly understand the AAFCO or National Research Council recommendations, yet many people profess knowledge and make erroneous proclamations.

"When you add [unproven] supplements, it's like you're taking a ride in an airplane that's been built in someone's garage that was designed by someone who isn't an aeronautical engineer and hasn't been tested," Dr. Carey says. "I don't know about you, but I wouldn't do it."

Dr. Downing believes certain supplements may be advantageous but cautions dog owners: "There is no safe, one-size-fits-all supplement. When supplementing, you need to individually tailor the supplementation to the particular animal. This is best accomplished through your veterinarian."

A Musher's Best Advice: Feed a Quality Diet

Unlike pets, hard-working sled dogs who run distance races such as the Yukon Quest and Iditarod or are in heavy sprint competition may require supplementation. Most mushers feed their dogs a diet specially formulated with the help of veterinary nutritionists, or they feed super-premium dog food with limited supplementation under a veterinarian's guidance.

"I do supplement with vitamin E," says Scott Chesney, a distance musher in Fairbanks, Alaska, who owns Siberian and Alaskan Huskies, the latter a type of dog bred for sled racing. "A few select dogs get probiotics [so-called good bacteria] and a couple get zinc. The probiotics and zinc are intended to clear up discoid lupus and were recommended by my vet."

Studies have shown that sled dogs who receive Vitamin E are more likely to finish long distance races than those who don't receive the supplementation. For details, see the May 2001 issue of Medicine and Science in Sports and Exercise.

Chesney's veterinarian and a veterinary ophthalmologist recommended vitamin E for certain dogs in his kennel. "You have to have an idea what you're doing [with Vitamin E]," the musher says.

His advice to the pet owner and even the performance dog owner who isn't training for long distance races is to feed a quality diet.

"If you feed a good quality food, you don't need to supplement." Visitors at his kennel often remark about his dogs' gorgeous coats, he says.

Chenesy believes that his dogs' beautiful coats are the result of feeding a super-premium dog food. In his opinion, "You feed the good stuff, and you don't have to worry about coats."

Preventing Deficiencies

Most pet owners think in terms of vitamin or mineral deficiencies, not balances or overdosing. However, balancing vitamins and minerals is equally as important as preventing a deficiency. Certain minerals, most notably calcium and phosphorus, must be balanced in ratios of 1 to 1 up to 2 to 1 to avoid leaching calcium from the bones. If either side of the ratio is too high, it can cause serious bone problems.

Common vitamin and mineral supplements include calcium, vitamin C, vitamin E, glucosamine, and Omega-3 fatty acids. Giving too much of a particular vitamin or mineral can inhibit the absorption of other vitamins or minerals.

"The challenge facing the pet owner is that the results aren't immediate," Dr. Carey says. "The malnutrition may be subtle, especially when it comes to the immune system or a serious imbalance. It may take a long time to manifest itself and even then, the pet owner might think the problems might be caused by another deficiency.

At Iams, we can test the immune system or perform bone density tests on dogs, something the pet owner usually can't do."

In general, if your veterinarian finds dietary deficiencies in your dog and advises supplements, use them. Otherwise, there is no need to supplement your dog's diet. ■

27

Fatty Foods

You're not doing your dog any favors
by "treating" with rich, fatty table scraps.

W hen your dog turns up his or her nose at the usual dog
food fare, it's tempting to dress up the dish with cheese,
milk, chicken broth and leftovers to encourage bowl-
cleaning. However well intentioned your gesture, it
actually may endanger the animal's health.

The addition of fatty foods to a dog's diet may increase the likelihood that the dog will become obese and may aggravate pancreatitis, or inflammation of the pancreas. The pancreas is a V-shaped
organ on the right side of the abdomen between the stomach and
the duodenum, the beginning of the small intestine. Among its critical functions, it produces:

■ hormones such as insulin to control metabolism and blood
sugar levels

■ enzymes to help digest food

■ other enzymes to protect the gland itself from self-absorption

Normally, the digestive enzymes become activated in the small
intestine. If they're activated within the pancreas, the gland begins
digesting its own tissue. The enzymes may even start to digest surrounding fat in the abdomen.

"Pancreatitis can be very serious," says Mary Labato, veterinary internist at Tufts University School of Veterinary Medicine. "It can run
the gamut from mild to life threatening and be the cause of rapid death."

The disease has two forms: acute and chronic. "Acute pancre-

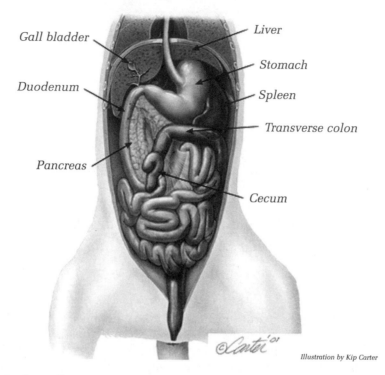

Gall bladder

Duodenum

Pancreas

Liver

Stomach

Spleen

Transverse colon

Cecum

Illustration by Kip Carter

atitis is the inflammation of the pancreas that occurs abruptly with little or no permanent pathologic change," Dr. Labato says. "Acute necrotizing [self-digesting] pancreatitis is a life threatening disease that can lead to acute renal failure, pleural effusion (fluid accumulated in the chest cavity) and death. Chronic pancreatitis is a continuing inflammatory disease that is often accompanied by irreversible changes."

Dogs may be vulnerable to pancreatitis at any age but it is most commonly seen in those seven years and older, Dr. Labato says. "And female dogs seem to be more regularly represented." Certain breeds seem more susceptible, including Miniature Schnauzers, Yorkshire and Silky Terriers, Miniature Poodles, and Cocker Spaniels.

In addition to fatty foods, causes include obesity, elevated levels of lipids (insoluble compounds of fats) in the blood, disease, injury as might occur in a car accident, and medications such as steroids.

While the cause cannot always be pinpointed, Dr. Joerg Steiner, a clinical assistant professor at Texas A&M College of Veterinary Medicine, says there typically is a spike in pancreatitis during the Thanksgiving and Christmas holidays because of owners' feeding rich foods like turkey skins and gravy to their dogs.

“ DOGS MAY BE VULNERABLE TO
PANCREATITIS AT ANY AGE BUT IS
MOST COMMONLY SEEN IN THOSE
SEVEN YEARS AND OLDER. ”

Watching for Symptoms

Dogs with the disease often will vomit and have abdominal pain. "They appear uncomfortable, sensitive to touch and may vocalize," says Dr. Steiner. Other signs range from mild to dramatic, including weight loss, panting, diarrhea, fever, depression, shock, and collapse. Affected dogs may stand with arched backs or lie with their rears in the air.

"This disease mimics and can be mimicked by almost any acute gastrointestinal disorder as well as a variety of extra-intestinal diseases," says Colin Burrows, a professor of medicine at the University of Florida College of Veterinary Medicine. Pancreatitis can resemble acute gastroenteritis, exacerbations of inflammatory bowel disease, peritonitis and acute renal failure, he says.

Veterinarians' diagnostic tools include a complete blood count and an evaluation of the pancreatic enzymes to determine if they're elevated, a sign of the disease's early stages. They may do additional blood tests, looking for elevated levels of other substances indicating the disease, and order X-rays and a CAT scan.

Increasingly, veterinarians are also using ultrasound to support the diagnosis of pancreatitis. "Unlike X-rays, which give only a general impression, ultrasound allows a thorough examination of the whole organ," Dr. Burrows says. "It is important to note, however, that a normal-appearing pancreas on ultrasound makes the diagnosis of pancreatitis less likely but most certainly does not eliminate it."

Treatment

Because dogs suffering pancreatitis are usually unable to keep down medications and food, they're hospitalized and given injectable medications and intravenous fluids. Veterinarians treat mild cases by preventing pancreatic stimulation, allowing no food or liquids for up to seventy-two hours. They also may administer anti-inflammatories, antibiotics, and pain and anti-nausea medicine.

"Dogs with diabetes that develop pancreatitis are difficult to treat," Dr. Labato says. "Their blood sugars may become very high." If insulin is given, the blood sugars will require close monitoring because the dog may become hypoglycemic. In addition, diabetes may result as complication of a severe case of pancreatitis.

Dogs with obstructions, a pancreatic abscess or mass may undergo surgery, although they're at greater risk for complications.

Complications of the disease alone can include irregular heartbeat, abnormal bleeding and breathing difficulties. Decreased enzyme production can also result from chronic pancreatitis, requiring the owner to add enzyme tablets or powder to the dog's food each day.

In most cases of pancreatitis, if the attack was mild and the dog had only one episode, chances recovery are good. In cases of acute necrotizing pancreatitis, the prognosis is guarded to poor, Dr. Labato says.

"The recovery rate really depends on the degree of severity of the attack," Dr. Steiner says. "In mild forms it is 100 percent recovery."

Often, affected dogs must be put on a prescription diet, avoiding high-protein and high-fat diets. Small, frequent feedings of a bland diet is the ideal, Dr. Labato says. Fatty table scraps are forbidden. And, much as it's tempting to give your dog those special treats, that's good advice for all owners, even those whose animals don't exhibit signs of pancreatic problems today. ■

28

Appetite for the Unusual

*There aren't many items that one
dog or another hasn't tried to eat. Learn
about possible causes and motivations
as well as ways to deter this behavior.*

Sticks, stones, paper, grass, leather—you name it, and a dog has probably eaten it or tried to eat it. Pica is the scientific word for eating abnormal stuff. Even more graphic—and to us repugnant—is a form of pica, known as coprophagy, the behavior of eating feces. Yes, some dogs eat it, their own as well as that of other dogs and other species such as cats, deer and horses.

The key word in the definition of pica is "abnormal." What may seem abnormal to us may be quite normal to dogs or, more specifically, to the dog in question. Pica becomes a problem only when the behavior becomes a physical risk to the dog or damages the relationship between the dog and the owner.

While shredding an occasional fetch stick isn't a big deal, chewing on wood can become a problem if it's obsessive and results in splinters, possible obstructions and lead poisoning if the wood has been covered with lead-based paints.

Why Do They Do It?

Behaviorists and other scientists cite a number of possible causes for this sometimes benign, sometimes life-threatening behavior. Nutritional causes are sometimes suspected, especially deficiencies in some trace minerals such as zinc and iron.

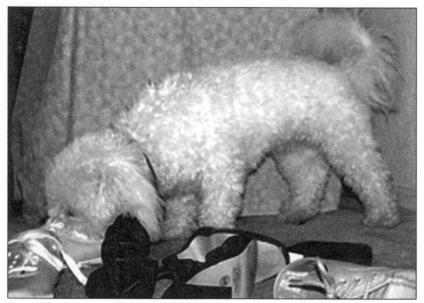

*Boredom and stress can lead dogs to put their dogs—and mouths—
where they don't belong.*

An emotional component may also be at work. Fearful, anxious, stressed, or bored dogs often resort to digging and chewing to resolve their discomfort. Their chewing can evolve into persistent and destructive habits to such a degree they practice pica behavior.

Finally, pica may be attention-getting behavior. Some dogs learn the quickest way to get their owners' attention is to grab and maybe chew on an object the owner considers important. They don't do this out of spite but because they're rewarded for the behavior by gaining the owner's attention. Rewarded behaviors tend to increase, and the pica worsens.

In the case of feces-eating dogs, there is some evidence the behavior may be related to a deficiency in a dog's naturally occurring digestive enzymes. However, some dogs actually enjoy the smell and taste of animal waste.

It's important to remember that what we call pica and coprophagy may be entirely normal behaviors from the dog's perspective. Dogs are naturally scavengers and opportunistic feeders. If something looks like food to them, it is food, even if it's something we would consider totally inappropriate, such as a book, shoe or purse. Leather is, after all, the skin of a dead animal, and dogs naturally eat dead animals.

Normal or not, some pica behavior can harm dogs. Since they have to live in human culture, and we want them to be safe and healthy, how do we deal with it?

Pica Prevention

Behavior management is an important part of pica prevention. Most eating habits are formed during a dog's puppyhood and adolescence. The use of crates, pens, leashes, tethers, and proper supervision can go a long way toward preventing pica, as can the ready availability of appropriate chew objects. Regular removal of stools from the pup's primary confinement area can forestall feces-eating.

If you can get through your dog's first year or two by directing chewing and eating to appropriate stuff, you will face little likelihood that the animal will develop pica and coprophagy habits as an adult. The exception is the eating of other species' feces—dogs do seem to be eternally attracted to that behavior, even if prevented from doing so as pups.

Breaking the Habit

If your dog already exhibits pica behavior, here are some strategies that may help to end or limit the behavior:

- **Have your veterinarian give your dog a complete physical** to rule out medical conditions that may contribute to the problem.
- **Take your dog out for breaks on leash.** Distract the animal from eating his or her own feces by providing praise or a treat or offering a toy or a rousing game of fetch.
- **Keep your yard scrupulously clean** of dog and other animal waste.
- **Feed your dog twice a day rather than once,** and include good sources of fiber in the animal's meal to give him or her a satisfied, full feeling.
- **Step up your pet's exercise program.** A tired dog is less likely to have the energy or desire to go on a feces hunt, and more exercise also will benefit your own health.
- **Add one of several deterrent products on the market to your dog's food.** Some are chewable tablets, available at retail and online pet stores. They work to stop coprophagy in some dogs, not for others, and it doesn't work, of course, to keep them from eating the feces of other animals.

■ **Apply a topical deterrent such as bitter apple or citronella to feces.** Again, this will work for some dogs, not for others.

■ **Keep your dog away from tempting sources.** Avoid areas where horse, cow, sheep, or deer dung are likely to be found. Make cat litter boxes inaccessible.

■ **Keep your cool.** It may be disgusting to watch your canine pal wolf down feces, but yelling at him or her won't help. If anything, it will teach your dog to carry out this habit surreptitiously so he or she won't get in trouble or to run away from you when you catch him in flagrante delicto. And remember, yelling is attention, even if it is negative attention, so you may unintentionally be encouraging the habit. If you find your dog in the process of sneaking an unacceptable snack, simply reinforce your commitment to manage the behavior. ■

Appendix

These groups and organizations were cited in this book. Their names and Web sites follow for readers who desire more information.

- American Animal Hospital Association: **www.aahanet.org**.
- American Boarding Kennels Association: **www.abka.com**.
- American Heartworm Society: **www.heartwormsociety.org**.
- American Kennel Club: **www.akc.org**.
- American Pet Products Manufacturers Association: **www.appma.org**.
- American Red Cross: **www.redcross.org**.
- American Society for the Prevention of Cruelty to Animals: **www.aspca.org**.
- American Veterinary Dental Society: **www.avds-online.org**.
- American Veterinary Medical Association: **www.avma.org**.
- Association of American Feed Control Officials: **www.aafco.org**.
- Centers for Disease Control and Prevention: **www.cdc.gov**.
- Food and Drug Administration: **www.fda.gov**.
- Humane Society of the United States: **www.hsus.org**.
- International Air Transport Association: **www.iata.org**.
- National Association of Professional Pet Sitters: **www.petsitters.org**.
- Pet Sitters International: **www.petsit.com**.
- Senior Dogs Project: **www.srdogs.com**.

These books were cited as references. For ordering information, contact the publisher or your favorite bookstore.

- *Balance Your Dog: Canine Massage* by C. Sue Furman (Wolfchase Publishing)
- *Caring for Your Dog: The Complete Canine Home Reference* by Bruce Fogle (DK Publishing)
- *The Complete Guide to Lost Pet Prevention and Recovery* by Joseph Andrew Sapia and Patricia Sapia (Atlantic Highlands)
- *The Dog Who Loved Too Much: Tales, Treatments, and the Psychology of Dogs* by Nicholas H. Dodman (Bantam)
- *KISS Guide to Raising a Puppy* by Liz Palika (DK Publishing)

Index